D1610499

REIMAGINING GLOBAL ABORTION POLITICS

A social justice perspective

Fiona Bloomer, Claire Pierson
and Sylvia Estrada Claudio

First published in Great Britain in 2019 by

Policy Press
University of Bristol
1-9 Old Park Hill
Bristol
BS2 8BB
UK
t: +44 (0)117 954 5940
pp-info@bristol.ac.uk
www.policypress.co.uk

North America office:
Policy Press
c/o The University of Chicago Press
1427 East 60th Street
Chicago, IL 60637, USA
t: +1 773 702 7700
f: +1 773-702-9756
sales@press.uchicago.edu
www.press.uchicago.edu

British Library Cataloguing in Publication Data
A catalogue record for this book is available from the British Library

Library of Congress Cataloging-in-Publication Data
A catalog record for this book has been requested

ISBN 978-1-4473-4043-0 hardcover
ISBN 978-1-4473-4044-7 ePDF
ISBN 978-1-4473-4046-1 ePub
ISBN 978-1-4473-4047-8 Mobi

Cover design by Hayes Design
Front cover image: www.emmacampbell.co.uk
Printed and bound in Great Britain by CPI Group (UK) Ltd,
Croydon, CR0 4YY
Policy Press uses environmentally responsible print partners

This book is dedicated to the thousands who lost their lives, to those whose lives have been impacted by poor access to abortion and to all those who have fought for abortion access.

Contents

Glossary

CEDAW	Convention on the Elimination of All Forms of Discrimination Against Women
ECHR	European Convention on Human Rights
ECtHR	European Court of Human Rights
ICCPR	International Covenant on Civil and Political Rights
ICWRSA	International Campaign for Women's Right to Safe Abortion
IPPF	International Planned Parenthood Federation
UDHR	Universal Declaration of Human Rights
WHO	World Health Organization
WOW	Women on Web

Notes on the authors

Fiona Bloomer, Ulster University, Lecturer in Social Policy.

Dr Bloomer's research centres on reproductive health, with a particular focus on abortion policy and abortion stigma. She is currently a co-investigator on a Global Challenges Research Fund seed fund project, 'Tackling Girls and Young Women's Reproductive Health through a Reproductive Justice Framework in the Philippines and South Africa', and in 2017 completed a groundbreaking study on abortion as a workplace issue.

Dr Bloomer's research findings have been published in international journals including *Culture, Health and Sexuality*, *Health and Human Rights*, *Critical Social Policy*, *Education, Citizenship and Social Justice*, and *Race Ethnicity and Education*. She is co-editor of a collection of papers published in 2018 exploring access to abortion in Ireland (north and south) and Prince Edward Island (Canada). She has secured funding awards from the British Academy, the Open Society Foundation, ACSONI/ROSA Foundation, Department for the Economy, and Unite the Union. Dr Bloomer is a founding member of the Reproductive Health Law and Policy Advisory Group, and a member of RAARN, the Reproductive Activism and Abortion Rights Network, a global network of academics and activists. Twitter: @DrBloomer

Claire Pierson, University of Liverpool, Lecturer in Politics.

Dr Pierson's research focuses on the UN women, peace and security agenda; conflict transformation; and reproductive rights and activism. She is currently a co-investigator on the project 'Tackling Girls and Young Women's Reproductive Health through a Reproductive Justice Framework in the Philippines and South Africa', and a unique research project funded by a coalition of Irish trade unions, addressing 'Abortion as a workplace issue on the island of Ireland'. Claire is co-founder of the Reproductive Health Law and Policy Advisory Group (https:// reproductivehealthlawpolicy.wordpress.com). She has published in journals including *The British Journal of Politics and International Relations*, *Parliamentary Affairs*, *The International Feminist Journal of Politics*, and *Nationalism and Ethnic Politics*. Prior to working in academia, Claire worked for the Atlantic Philanthropies, the Institute for Conflict Research (Belfast) and the Palestinian Human Rights Monitoring Group (Jerusalem).

Sylvia Estrada Claudio, Dean of the College of Social Work and Community Development (CSWCD), University of the Philippines, Professor of the CSWCD's Department of Women and Development Studies.

Dr Claudio is a doctor of medicine who also holds a PhD in Psychology. She is a graduate of the University of the Philippines College of Medicine and earned her PhD in Philippine Psychology from University of the Philippines Diliman. She also did a postgraduate research fellowship at the University of Amsterdam in 1990.

She is the author of several publications, including the books *Rape love and sexuality: The construction of women in discourse* (UP Press, 2002) and *And then she laughed: Counseling women* (Anvil Press, 2015).

She considers herself an engaged academic because she has spent most of her life working in the Philippine and international social movements. She started in her teens when she was part of the underground movement against the Marcos dictatorship. Her longest-standing major engagement is that she is co-founder, and now Chair, of the Board of Directors of Likhaan, an organisation working with grassroots women on issues of reproductive and sexual health and rights. She is also a member of the Philippine Psychological Association's LGBT Special Interest Group, a lifetime member of the Pambansang Samahan ng Sikolohiyang Pilipino (National Association of Philippine Psychology), and a member of the Council of Asian Association of Women's Studies.

For the past 30 years, she has been providing free counselling services to women and LGBT survivors of violence.

Her areas of research interest are sexuality and development, political and movement theories, sexual and reproductive health and rights, feminist and LGBT psychology, violence against women, religious fundamentalisms, universal healthcare, women and ICT.

Acknowledgements

As a collective, the authors would like to express their heartfelt thanks to all who made this book possible: those fighting for abortion rights, whether as advocates or service providers, who have inspired us to pursue our research interests. We are in awe of the risks many of you take in order to save women's lives and uphold women's dignity. It is your work that we wish to spotlight and honour in this book.

We also wish to thank colleagues who were sounding boards: Mara Clarke, Deirdre Duffy, Marlene Gerber Fried, Rachel Monaghan, Jennifer Thomson, Kellie O'Dowd, Marisa Viana, Katie Gillum, Marge Berer, Stephen Bloomer, and Susan Yanow and also those who provided time away from other responsibilities to allow us to dedicate time and energy to the book. Particular thanks go Emma Campbell who was not only a sounding board but also conducted a thorough read-through of the final draft.

To those who were interviewed for the publication, we express our thanks; we have huge respect for your work and are grateful for the time you gave to us.

We would like to thank members of the ethics committee at Ulster University who scrutinised the project plan for the publication and provided ethical approval for the primary fieldwork.

Our thanks also go to the Gynuity Health Projects, for permitting reproduction of the table 'Countries where mifepristone is registered/ licensed' and the 'Global map of countries where Misoprostol is approved'.

Finally, we would like to thank Emma Campbell, whose work *An Appropriate Hobby: Passport Butterfly Photos of Activists* features on the front cover of the book. Emma's work can be found at www. emmacampbell.co.uk

ONE

Introduction

Throughout the twentieth century and into the twenty-first, abortion has moved from being a largely private and ungoverned matter to one which has been highly politicised. Such politicisation is multidimensional, incorporating the belief in a fundamental argument or polarisation on the issue of who can authorise abortions, why they are permitted and where they are licensed to take place. Politicisation is influenced by social, cultural, institutional and historical factors, yet throughout a range of societies we can see at its core the issue of power and how it relates to gender regimes in specific contexts. Politicisation also has the potential to mobilise, as individual experience is recognised as collective and activism for such collective experience ensues. These arguments, issues and experiences are the focus of this book. Our objective is to demonstrate and analyse this politicisation in a variety of global contexts with the aim of highlighting commonalities, differences and ultimately the factors and discourses which shape women's access to, and experience of, abortion.

The authorship team came together to write this book as we recognised that there was a significant gap in the synthesis of the literature examining global trends in abortion politics. We recognised the need to provide a critical, comparative analysis of contemporary issues within the Global North and South, and to construct a schema of international abortion politics. We understood that current regressions and progressions in abortion politics cannot be viewed in isolation, and so we have also sought to provide a brief historical narrative of the development of abortion law and policy in the twentieth century. We have considered data which allows for identification of trends in abortion access, with a particular focus on unsafe abortion. Interviews with activists, advocates, abortion funders and providers explore these trends from a range of perspectives. The book identifies that while abortion law and policy is constantly changing in national contexts, there are a number of common discourses informing debates and subsequently women's access to abortion.

Each member of the writing team has brought their own expertise and knowledge to the publication, and we have learned from each other throughout the process. Our ultimate goal was to present a feminist, critical analysis of abortion politics that would be of interest

1

to scholars, activists and policy makers, and that would identify factors that enable or challenge access to abortion and consider perspectives from the Global North and South.

The book as a whole is informed by a social justice perspective and recognises that academic approaches aid us in understanding the laws, policies and discourses that shape abortion politics, however this is also an issue of human rights, equality and social justice which impacts on women's reproductive lives globally, in terms of both their public and their intimate citizenship. Consequently, while this book hopes to inform and provide a unique contribution to academic perspectives and analysis, it also works on the basis that this understanding will ultimately contribute to global social change regarding women's bodily autonomy and rights.

Before commencing with an overview of the book, we each reflect on why we began this writing project.

Fiona Bloomer

My primary motivation for writing about abortion politics stems from my work exploring abortion policy over the last decade. Before I focused my academic interests on abortion and reproductive health more broadly, my work had centred on social justice issues in Northern Ireland. It was evident from this work that structural inequalities were experienced differently by women; by those from lesbian, gay, bisexual and trans communities; by those in lower socioeconomic groups; and by people of colour. The intersection of all of these was largely not recognised by the state. In the latter part of 2008, I became aware of the work of the activist group Alliance for Choice, following an introduction by my dear friend Kellie O'Dowd. During 2008, an opportunity had arisen to bring the archaic abortion legislation in Northern Ireland, which dates from 1861, in line with the rest of the UK. Alliance for Choice had reinvigorated its support base in 2008, drawing in community and trade union activists to lobby for change, in order to reform a legal framework that rendered abortion almost impossible to access. The opportunity was hampered by opposition from the four main political parties, the main churches and a high-profile anti-abortion campaign. Political manoeuvring resulted in the campaign failing, and thus commenced a renewed strategic direction by Alliance for Choice to lobby for change, to bring on board allies and to improve the positioning of abortion in wider society. I have been fortunate over the last decade to observe at close quarters the concerted efforts of Alliance for Choice activists and the development of their campaign. These range from reactionary to proactive efforts, which have included taking an active role in legal challenges before the Northern Ireland courts, organising and leading consultation sessions on draft guidelines for medical professionals, engaging with political parties to help inform and educate party members on the restrictive law and its impact, engaging with the public through efforts such as information stalls and media appearances, and engaging with faith organisations who wished to challenge the assumption that people of faith are anti-abortion. In working with allies, Alliance for Choice has developed lasting, effective relationships with national reproductive health organisations; activist organisations regionally, nationally and internationally; student unions; and trade unions. It has also developed innovative community-based education programmes, as well as developed a significant profile in national and international media highlighting the injustices in abortion provision in Northern Ireland. It has centred artistic endeavours in its work, led by the talented Emma Campbell, who along with Kellie O'Dowd and a team of passionate activists has contributed to a more nuanced understanding of abortion in Northern Irish society.

My journey in researching abortion policy brought me into contact with some of those directly impacted by restrictive laws. In particular, Sarah Ewart and her mother, Jane Christie, and Ashleigh Topley, all of whom who have spent extensive time and effort tirelessly highlighting the injustices suffered by those denied abortion. Countless others have also shared their stories with me and helped me to understand the impact of an unjust, deeply flawed law and inadequate abortion provision. Many of these stories appear in the multimedia project #MyBodyMyLife, which, led by Lesley Hoggart, sought to challenge abortion stigma in the UK. Alongside those seeking abortions, those involved in abortion and broad reproductive health provision have been generous with their time and insight to enable me to understand issues impacting on how services are delivered, this includes individuals such as Dawn Purvis, Breedagh Hughes and Donagh Stenson. Mara Clarke, founder of Abortion Support Network, has been supremely patient with my inquiries about the complex cases that the organisation deals with and has introduced me to networks of activists, advocates and providers globally.

At the same time as my knowledge and understanding of abortion policy developed, I began working with Claire Pierson, when we discovered a common interest in abortion rights during a writing club which we established to support each other in our endeavours to get published. From this grew projects on political discourse and later, along with colleagues, we hosted the first international conference in the UK on abortion and reproductive justice. This conference, and its predecessor in Prince Edward Island, Canada, served to crystallise my thirst for knowledge about abortion access around the globe.

I am fortunate to have been provided with opportunities to study abortion access in several countries around the world. This has afforded me insight into how abortion is positioned in different societies, and how this impacts on law and access. In recent years, I have been extremely fortunate to meet with academics and activists who are leaders in their field and who have inspired me. In particular, Marlene Gerber Fried has been generous with her time, providing advice and guidance in my journey to understand reproductive justice, and she also introduced me to the passionate, indomitable academic activist Sylvia Estrada Claudio. More recently, the trade union leaders and activists involved in the groundbreaking study, 'Abortion as a Workplace Issue' (UNITE the Union, Unison, Mandate Trade Union, the CWU Ireland, the GMB, Trade Union Campaign to Repeal the 8th, Alliance for Choice), have enhanced my respect of the power of collective action and demonstrated how research can be utilised to provide a foundation for campaigns to reform restrictive abortion laws.

My direct experience of working with those affected by restrictive laws, activists and leading scholars in the field has shaped my research interests; and my thirst to understand how these laws and policies are formed, implemented, resisted and experienced, provided a foundation for the motivation to write this book.

Claire Pierson

My perspective on women's right to access abortion is informed by both my academic work and my experiences of working with women globally. Prior to working in academia, I worked internationally as a teacher of English for five years (in China, the Czech Republic and Egypt). During this time, I also volunteered for a number of organisations, including a Roma rights group and as a statement recorder for refugees and asylum seekers. This work informed my decision to complete a master's degree in human rights and subsequently to volunteer in Jerusalem for a Palestinian human rights organisation and in Belfast for a centre researching the effects of conflict on local communities.

During all of this experience it was obvious in the work that I was doing that women, though suffering the same human rights abuses as men, suffered added layers of discrimination and inequality based solely on gender identity. Between 2012 and 2015, while completing doctoral research in Northern Ireland on discourses of gender security in the region, I became aware that lack of access to abortion was rarely mentioned by women participating in my research. As a Northern Irish woman, I found it compelling that lack of access to reproductive rights was so silenced within women's narratives of security and inequality.

I was lucky to be invited to be involved in research with Fiona in 2015, which looked at the political discourse on abortion in Northern Ireland. Through this research, the stigmatisation and silencing of abortion through the overtly moralistic and conservative tone of political debate highlighted to me how women are really viewed by those who politically represent the electorate of Northern Ireland. Through this research, I became convinced that to really understand women's positioning in society and to argue for equality and justice the site of reproduction is a fundamental place to start from.

Since this, I have worked and published on a number of projects, including those on Irish women's experiences of travelling to England to access abortion services, Irish trade union members' views on abortion and legal reform, reproductive rights in crisis and conflict situations, and reproductive justice in the Philippines and South Africa. This has broadened my understanding of abortion and its connection to other inequalities and injustices in particular societies, which I hope has been expressed in this volume and contributes to the reader's understanding of the fundamental need to ensure women's freedom to control their reproductive lives.

Sylvia Estrada Claudio

In June 2016, I was invited to Ulster University in Belfast to speak at a conference entitled 'Abortion and Reproductive Justice: The Unfinished Revolution II'.

There I met Fiona Bloomer and Claire Pierson. I was particularly pleased by the conference because, among other things, it brought out so many perspectives on the issue of abortion that allowed us all to look at it in various frames that reflected the multifaceted realities of women. Fiona and Claire were among the group of activist-academics who ensured that concepts such as 'choice' or 'rights' were contextualised in women's struggle for justice. I was impressed that I, a woman who was coming from a country that has one of the most repressive abortion laws in the world and very little to show in terms of advocacy on this specific issue, should find a place in the conference.

Somehow, our 16-year struggle in the Philippines for a reproductive health law which avoided any discussion on changing the law on abortion, made sense. Somehow my (and other colleagues') history of working in the anti-dictatorship movement, delivering basic reproductive and sexual health services to poor communities and integrating health work into broader development frameworks, made sense.

Imagine, then, my greater pleasure when I was asked to join them in writing this book.

If being at that conference and integrating my realities into the discussions on abortion had been a challenge, it has been more so in writing this book. I have had to cross conceptual boundaries, decentre myself from my personal history and experience when necessary, and find connections to my context where they could be found.

Our easy and productive working relations are proof that when inclusive and integrative frameworks are brought to bear on an issue, new insights can be gained. Hopefully, this should prove helpful to scholars, activists and scholar-activists in different spaces, places and movements.

Working with Claire and Fiona has also taught me that political integrity lies not just in refusing to strip our issues of the contexts in which we live, but also in recognising the contexts of others. It is by recognising the convergences and divergences, the parallels that will never meet or the separations that may eventually becoming unifying, that we are best able to forge our strategies.

A note on terminology

Throughout this book we use the term 'women' to denote those who are of reproductive age and have the reproductive capacity to become pregnant. We wish to acknowledge from the outset that trans men are included in consideration of those that have the reproductive capacity to become pregnant and that trans men may experience additional barriers in accessing reproductive health services including abortion, as well as being subjected to discriminatory behaviours in society more broadly. The word 'women' is used for brevity, clarity and consistency but also to acknowledge that the majority of those wishing to access abortion are women.

Structure of the book

This book is divided into six main chapters, focusing on a range of themes integral to the politicisation of abortion, and which aim to provide insight and critical analysis into global abortion politics in the twenty-first century. These themes are criminalisation, biomedicalisation, abortion discourses (religion, culture, nation), international interventions, activism and reproductive justice. Within each chapter we present evidence identified through a review of the literature and interviews with key informants. Each chapter also includes case studies of individual countries or organisations to provide insight into the thematic areas, for instance, in analysing how culture and religion influences access to abortion in two different settings, one where a liberal legal framework exists and one where a restrictive framework exists.

The book begins by considering the criminalisation of abortion (Chapter Two). We highlight how a review of the history of the criminal law on abortion reveals that for most of history abortion remained outside the law. Criminalisation when it did occur was closely tied to the religious positioning of abortion in Western societies. This chapter considers trends in the latter part of the twentieth century, when countries which had criminalised abortion began to relax laws, while in other settings restrictions were introduced. The investigation of the impact of restrictive laws and restricted access includes an exploration of the data related to death and serious injury resulting from unsafe abortion, as well as the risk of criminality. A consideration of methodological issues in measuring the impact of unsafe abortion identifies new methods to quantify this. Case studies of the Republic of Ireland and Uruguay highlight how restrictive laws are experienced in contrasting settings. This chapter concludes by considering the case for decriminalisation of abortion.

In Chapter Three we move on to consider the development of the biomedicalisation of abortion. The recent history of the biomedicalisation of abortion reveals the key role played by pharmaceutical companies in the development of a medication to induce abortion (mifepristone) and how localised knowledge among women identified the abortifacient properties of a second medication (misoprostol). The chapter reflects on the expectations that the biomedicalisation of abortion would improve access and reduce the need for abortion to be accessed in clinical settings. Although the biomedicalisation of abortion was initially hailed as a way to put women at the centre of the process, the implementation was problematic.

The impact of commercial pressures on pharmaceutical companies is discussed, as well as challenges faced by those accessing the medication without adequate information on dosage and usage. The case study of Brazil highlights the hugely significant role played by women in communities experiencing multiple barriers to accessing abortion, in sharing knowledge about a medication which, having been developed for other purposes, became known for its abortifacient purposes. This case study also illustrates the challenges experienced by those seeking post-abortion care in restricted settings. The impact of the Zika virus in 2015 highlights how severe inadequacies within reproductive health policy affected women and their families. The chapter concludes by considering the impact of biomedicalisation on health professionals, and the changing dynamic in the relationship between the clinician and the woman seeking an abortion.

Chapter Four, 'Abortion discourses', explores the impact of cultural factors, values and norms, and their interaction with institutions, on how abortion is positioned in society. It considers the position that institutions do not operate in a vacuum but are influenced by the values and norms which make them part of the cultural fabric of a society. The ideologies that influence this are explored. The role of faith-based organisations in shaping international policy illustrates how religious norms shape conservatism and, alternatively, how liberal organisations challenge such norms. A consideration of transitional societies allows for an analysis of how abortion is positioned in a framework whereby cultural, national and religious norms typically influence conservative discourses. In such settings, gender rights become subservient to other rights or, alternatively, may become core to legal reform. Two case studies, Northern Ireland and South Africa, illustrate how abortion discourses are shaped in societies emerging from conflict and apartheid.

Chapter Five presents an analysis of international interventions and their role in challenging restricted access to abortion. The use of human rights treaties is considered. In this chapter, we also analyse how access to reproductive health is impacted in situations of conflict and humanitarian crisis. The role of CEDAW, the Convention on the Elimination of All Forms of Discrimination against Women, is considered with reference to a case study of the Philippines. This case study illustrates how access to contraception provided a driver for legal action in a setting where access to abortion was severely restricted, and how a post-abortion care policy has provided an alternative way to deal with unsafe abortion. Also explored is the impact of the 'global gag rule', which has restricted funding from the US to those working on reproductive health around the world. The case study of the International Planned Parenthood Federation (IPPF) and its work on humanitarian issues provides insight into the challenges faced in providing reproductive health services in settings where resources are extremely limited.

Chapter Six, 'Activism', centres the transnational work of activists around the globe whose goal is to improve access to abortion, to take action to provide or facilitate access, and to improve knowledge about and challenge stigma around abortion. We consider the recent history of abortion activism beginning with the Jane Collective, which operated primarily in the Chicago area of the US, providing access to abortion and abortion services during the late 1960s/early 1970s. This chapter reflects on how, in the twenty-first century, resistance to prohibitive legal frameworks and restricted access is offered by national and international organisations who work in collaboration with grassroots groups. The chapter reflects on the wide range of work carried out by activist organisations which provide short-term help or longer-term interventions to circumvent laws or change societal perceptions about abortion.

In Chapter Seven we reflect on the development of the Reproductive Justice Framework and how it is being applied internationally. We also reflect on the terminology used around reproductive justice and how this is impacted by different contexts such as the US and Argentina. A consideration of the choice framework is offered. The case study of RESURJ, an international organisation of young feminists working in the Global South, provides insight into how movements can work at grassroots and international levels, promoting the values of reproductive justice in order to improve the lives of those most affected by oppressive laws and policies. The chapter further considers how reproductive justice can shine a light on countries with multiple reproductive oppressions, such as Egypt. The chapter concludes by considering a recent development in the theoretical framework of reparative reproductive justice.

In Chapter Eight we draw together the themes from each main chapter and reflect on the stories we have uncovered during the process of writing this book. We consider what lies ahead in terms of challenges and opportunities, and identify what further research needs to be conducted.

Limitations

The content of this book reflects both the individual and the combined experiences of the authors, from positions which are grounded in the Global North and the Global South. The content of the book was shaped by our own research knowledge, extensive desk research and primary interviews with academics and activists from around the globe. The book only has scope to identify a number of international case studies, it could not possibly encompass all potential cases around the globe that provide a nuanced insight into abortion politics. However, our research approach was sufficiently robust to allow for identification of findings that can be applied to settings not included in the publication. We acknowledge that we have not addressed every issue that is impacted by abortion politics; debates on gender selection and disability and their use in abortion myths, for instance, have not been included. We have largely focused on abortion politics as it relates to women, though we recognise that girls may face additional issues because of their age, and trans men because of discrimination and additional barriers they face. Each chapter could warrant a book in itself. In the concluding chapter, we identify future directions for research and pose key questions that have yet to be fully explored.

TWO

Criminalisation

Abortion as a practice for ending pregnancy has been documented for thousands of years. Largely a private matter, often euphemistically known as 'menstrual regulation', knowledge of how to end a pregnancy has been passed between women and treated as a normal, if mostly secret, part of reproductive life for millennia. Legislative interference into abortion is a more modern phenomenon, and indicates changing perspectives and relationships towards the foetus, the control of women's bodies and the governance of medical procedures.

The status of abortion in national legal systems does not necessarily reflect easy access to the procedure. Issues of stigma, cost, location of clinics, restrictions on who can provide abortion services and gestational limits continue to affect women's access to safe abortion even in cases where the law appears liberal. However, it is clear that in regions where legal restrictions are in place, a number of added complications exist for women wishing to access abortion. These include accessing abortion away from regulated settings, and in doing so, risking unsafe abortion. Added complications include the need to pay for the abortion, which is often at a significant cost, having to travel to other jurisdictions, and most obviously the risk of prosecution if found to have procured an illegal abortion.

In some jurisdictions the increasingly draconian interpretation of abortion laws has seen women prosecuted for illegally procuring abortion pills (Northern Ireland) or imprisoned for having miscarriages (El Salvador). In other settings laws exist which completely criminalise any abortion procedure even where a woman's life is at risk (Malta, the Dominican Republic, Nicaragua), and lawmakers globally continue to put forward laws which will narrow the grounds on which abortion is legal (Poland, the United States).

This chapter considers the adoption of laws criminalising abortion and their effect on women's access to abortion. The case studies of the Republic of Ireland and Uruguay illustrate how women and healthcare providers have had to adapt to restrictive abortion laws and how restrictive laws do little to stop abortion from occurring. The chapter concludes by presenting the case for decriminalisation of abortion laws globally.

Criminalising abortion

The history of abortion dates back thousands of years. In ancient Greek and Roman times, the use of abortifacients such as *Ruta graveolens* (a medicinal herb) were commonly cited alongside medical procedures to remove the foetus akin to the modernday dilute and curettage (Riddle, 1999). Archival evidence from over 5,000 years ago suggests that women in China were advised to drink mercury to terminate a pregnancy. In many societies, abortions were provided by midwives in the community. Others performing abortions included doctors, vets, pharmacists, herbalists, lay health practitioners and masseurs (McLaren, 1978). Abortion was more recently commonly referred to as 'menstrual regulation' and was common practice in many societies. For example, newspapers and magazines in Britain (pre the Abortion Act 1967) show advertisements for tablets and herbal remedies to 'remove stubborn menstrual blockages' (Fisher, 1998). As discussed in Chapter Six, this positioning of abortion as 'menstrual regulation' has been in use in Bangladesh since 1979 as part of the National Family Planning Programme.

Abortion largely remained outside the interest of lawmakers for a considerable part of history, particularly when carried out before the point of quickening (the point at which the foetus was felt moving in the womb). A combination of conservative social views, increased medical knowledge of pregnancy, and medics seeking to restrict the activities of other practitioners led to increasing criminalisation of abortion in the nineteenth century (Rose, 2007). English law changed in 1803 to criminalise the act of abortion before the point of quickening, though it was not as severely punishable as after quickening (Cook, 2000). Following amendments in 1828 and 1837, abortion was incorporated in the Offences Against the Person Act 1861, Section 58 of which became the foundation of the criminalisation of abortion in many jurisdictions of the common law world (Cook, 2000). Following this, in 1869, the Roman Catholic Church redefined the mortal sin of abortion to apply not only from quickening but from conception, bringing secular criminal law and religious institutions' positions in line with each other.

It is clear that criminalisation contributed to conservative views on abortion, though this position was not universal. France, for instance, positioned abortion within the framework of family planning as a 'social practice' in the late nineteenth century, much earlier than other European countries. This was ascribed to a number of factors, the most common ones being the lack of effective contraceptive methods and the closure of foundling homes, where those facing crisis pregnancies had previously left newborns. Increased access to abortion in France occurred through the sharing of home-based abortion methods within women's informal networks, in communities and workplaces. In addition, an over-proliferation of midwives and doctors offering abortion services, alongside a view that abortion was safe, contributed to a widening acceptance of abortion. French feminist thinkers and medics articulated that emerging feminism was leading to increased recognition from women that they should have bodily autonomy (McLaren, 1978).

The French historical context is in contrast to jurisdictions where the criminalisation of abortion is rooted within societal expectations and control of women, pregnancy and motherhood, including pronatalist policies of authoritarian regimes (for example, Romania and Chile) and the controlling dominance of conservative religious institutions (for example, Ireland and Latin America). Notably, the situation in France dramatically changed just after World War I when natalist policies were implemented to compensate for the heavy loss in population. In 1920 for instance legislation was introduced that prohibited abortion and material that promoted contraception. The most significant legal reforms addressing restrictions occurred in 1967 with the introduction of the Neuwirth Law, allowing the use of contraceptives and then in 1975 the Veil Law legalising abortion (interview with Jean Guilleminot, Hôpitaux Universitaires Paris Ouest, 2018).

Abortion law in the twentieth and twenty-first centuries

By the latter part of the twentieth century, the trend for liberalisation of abortion laws was well established within most of the Global North and Central and East Asia (Rahman et al, 1998; Boland and Katzive, 2008; Finer and Fine, 2013). Modern developments in abortion law have moved away from punishment towards women's health needs. Further to this, a rights-based approach to abortion has emerged based on bodily self-determination and the right to healthcare. However, abortion remains a crime in many countries and highly restricted in many others, largely those in the continents of South America and Africa.

Regressive steps have been introduced in some countries to restrict access. These include replacing a liberal law with restrictive law (for example, Poland) or introducing procedural steps such as flawed/biased counselling, extended waiting periods, mandatory vaginal ultrasounds, involvement of pregnant teens' parents and limiting private insurance coverage for the procedure (for example, in some US states such as Texas), all of which seek to place additional barriers to those seeking abortion (Finer and Fine, 2013). A study of the impact of restrictions in Texas identified that clinic closures led to additional logistics for those seeking abortions as well as increased financial costs. For instance, it was identified that there was a substantial increase in the mean distance women had to travel, from 22 miles one way to 85 miles. Those who travelled more than 50 miles incurred costs to do so, typically more than $100; in sum, access to abortion to became extremely problematic (Gerdts et al, 2016). Between 2010 and 2017, such restrictions came in close succession, with over 300 applied throughout the US (Nash et al, 2017).

Globally, legal frameworks for accessing abortion fall into four broad categories, from most to least restrictive, as classified by the Center for Reproductive Rights (2018). Category I laws are the most restrictive laws, which either prohibit abortion entirely or permit it only to save a woman's life. It is estimated that 25% of the world's population resides in the 66 countries with such laws. These countries are mostly located in the Global South (El Salvador, the Dominican Republic and Nicaragua). Malta is the only EU country which bans abortion in all cases.

The second most restrictive category permits abortion to protect a woman's life and health. The 59 countries in this category are scattered throughout the world and comprise about 14% of the world's population. The laws of most Category II countries authorise abortion on 'health' or 'therapeutic' grounds. Some of the laws in these countries specify the gravity of the possible injury and only permit abortion if the potential harm is grave, serious or permanent. Alternatively, some laws, such as those of Zimbabwe and Monaco, specify that abortion is available only if the physical health of a woman is in danger. Others, such as those in force in Colombia and Ghana, permit abortion if a woman's mental or physical health is at risk.

In the third category are those countries that expand on the reasons in category two to allow abortion for socioeconomic reasons. These countries are spread throughout the world and encompass approximately 21% of the world's population. In practice, these abortion laws are usually interpreted liberally and allow women to obtain abortions because of factors such as their age, economic status or marital status. Generally, socioeconomic reasons for abortion are considered within the framework of women's health. For example, the laws of Britain (England, Scotland and Wales), Belize and Zambia consider a woman's 'actual or reasonably foreseeable environment' in determining whether the pregnancy endangers her physical or mental health.

The fourth category are those countries with the most liberal abortion laws (61 in total). These countries comprise 40% of the world's population. They are located primarily in the Global North, and include most countries in North America, Europe and Central and East Asia (including China, the world's most populous country). These countries permit abortion without restriction as to reason and prioritise women within decision-making about terminating a pregnancy. Within this category are countries which have removed abortion from criminal law and moved it into the health arena. Canada presents as an exemplifier of one such country. While abortion was legalised in Canada in 1969, this was governed by a set of restrictions which impacted significantly on access. These restrictions were overturned in 1988 by the Canadian Supreme Court following a challenge by the medic Dr Henry Morgentaler, who had long argued that access to abortion should not be subject to approval by committees and not only provided in hospital settings. The Supreme Court judgment resulted in federal restrictions on abortion being removed and decriminalisation (Erdman, 2018). The impact of this judgement was that abortion was firmly positioned as part of healthcare and made available on request in hospital and clinic settings.

However, even when abortion is decriminalised, access can remain problematic for some. For example, in Canada abortion is inaccessible or restricted in the Maritime Provinces, northern regions and rural areas. On Prince Edward Island, in the Atlantic coast area, abortion services were largely unavailable until 2016. This restricted access resulted from insular geography, a prevailing anti-abortion lobby movement and a passive provincial government (Bloomer et al, 2018a: 12). Even when liberal laws provide a framework for access, this alone does not guarantee ready access to abortion; stigma, availability of clinics and other contributory factors can hamper access. South Africa presents as a classic example of this, where stigma about abortion and poor infrastructure are barriers to access, as illustrated in Chapter Four on abortion discourses.

The result of criminalising abortion

The result of restricting abortion access is not that it stops abortion happening. In fact, data suggests that where abortion is illegal, abortion rates are higher. For example, the abortion rate during the time period 2010–14 in South America, where restricted laws are typical, was estimated at 47 per 1,000 women of childbearing age, whereas in Western Europe, where most countries have liberal laws, the abortion rate was 18 per 1,000 (Sedgh et al, 2016). These statistics must be considered in conjunction with evidence of inadequate sexual health and relationship education, and inadequate access to contraception, within countries with high abortion rates.

The main effects of restrictive legislation are to make abortion unsafe, and to push women to travel to neighbouring jurisdictions to access abortion or to risk criminality by accessing abortions away from regulated settings. These effects are generally felt more by women made vulnerable by their socioeconomic and residency status.

The World Health Organization (WHO) (2012) estimates that of the 44 million abortions performed globally each year, 21.6 million women experience an unsafe abortion. Unsafe abortions are defined by the WHO as 'a procedure for terminating an unwanted pregnancy either by persons lacking the necessary skills or in an environment lacking the minimal medical standards, or both' (WHO, 2003).

Calculating the exact numbers of unsafe abortions poses challenges for researchers, due to recording and methodological issues. Three major studies have reported on unsafe abortion data with respect to maternal deaths:

1. A WHO publication that considered data from 2008 estimated that 13% (47,000) of all maternal deaths globally could be attributed to unsafe abortion (WHO, 2011).
2. A WHO study that considered data from the period 2003–09 estimated that abortion–related deaths accounted for 7.9% (193,000) of maternal deaths (Say et al, 2014).
3. A study by the Institute for Health Metrics and Evaluation estimated that 14.9% (43,684) of all maternal deaths globally in 2013 could be attributed to unsafe abortion as well as causes related to abortion (Kassebaum et al, 2014).

The WHO study of the 2008 data is widely used, having been cited over 900 times. The publication of the latter two studies in 2014 has caused some consternation among observers (Berer et al, 2016). Both have adopted robust, methodologically sound approaches, but they differ considerably, making comparisons problematic. Nor can the WHO study of 2011 be readily compared with the 2014 study. This presents a problem for researchers and policy makers – which source provides the most accurate estimate? A consensus has yet to be reached; however, as the Institute for Health Metrics and Evaluation study

(Kassebaum et al, 2014) provides a more comprehensive approach, it is this study that will be adopted by the authors here.

Unsafe abortion is one of the leading causes of maternal mortality (14.9%) (Kassebaum et al, 2014). Of the women who survive unsafe abortion, it is estimated that 5 million will suffer long-term health complications such as infertility, internal organ damage or psychological harm (Haddad and Nour, 2009). In countries where abortion is legal, maternal morbidity and mortality are generally lower because abortions are performed by/regulated by trained professionals and are safer, more available and more affordable.

For those who cannot readily access abortion close to home, the option to travel may be pursued. Abortion travel is a global phenomenon (Sethna and Doull, 2012). This travel can be across national borders (for example, from the Republic of Ireland to England or from Poland to Germany) or within country borders (for example, from Prince Edward Island to mainland Canada or between states in the US). Despite abortion travel rarely being conceptualised as part of the 'medical tourism' field, it is clearly linked, with both involving travel to circumvent legal and extra-legal impediments to services (Sethna and Doull, 2012). However, the term 'tourism' implies some form of freedom and choice, and such freedom is not conveyed by abortion travel (Cresswell, 2010). Fletcher (2013) illustrates how such travel can make the governance of abortion services 'peripheral' (in the Irish context) and results in official tolerance for the act of abortion as long as it is not performed within the state.

The problematic nature of abortion travel is often conceptualised with regard to the practical factors such as cost and logistics involved in such travel and the gendered inequality that is the result. This analysis is of crucial importance, but it seldom analyses the actual care that women are given and receive on these journeys. An assumption is made that women receive safe care, but less is known about the dynamics and quality of this care. However, recent studies of healthcare professionals in Ireland (Aiken et al, 2017a; Duffy and Pierson, 2017) indicate that travel creates health risks, particularly for women who already have health issues.

Access to the abortion pill from telemedicine providers such as Safe2Choose, Women on Web (WOW) and Women Help Women has provided alternative means to access abortion without the need to travel. Studies reporting on Women on Web clients indicate that during a five-year period (2010–15) 5,650 women in the Republic of Ireland and Northern Ireland requested medication through Women on Web. The data provides some insight into the level of demand for services (Aiken et al, 2017b).

Safe2Choose, Women on Web and Women Help Women operate on the model of telemedicine, whereby an online consultation process is offered to women seeking abortion. This consultation process screens for suitability for the medication, including identification of contraindications and risk factors for potential complications:

> Women are advised to have an ultrasound to confirm the gestation and to exclude an ectopic pregnancy. During the online consultation and in subsequent emails, the women are informed about complications, circumstances when they should seek additional medical assistance, what to do in case of a continuing pregnancy, and future contraceptive options. Responses to the questionnaire are reviewed by a doctor. If necessary, additional questions or advice is given by email or telephone. A helpdesk in the five languages of the website answers emails seven days a week. (Gomperts et al. 2008: 1172, explaining the WOW process)

If the woman is assessed as suitable, medication is then sent by post to her address or the address of an intermediary (usually an activist). Detailed instructions are provided on administration of the medication, including what to do if the woman is concerned about excessive bleeding or other complications. Online follow-up assessments are conducted by Women on Web staff within five weeks. In recent years, the organisation has expanded its activities and now provides information about abortion medication in 17 different languages.

In restricted jurisdictions information about telemedicine providers is typically shared within networks, social media and information campaigns such as stickers/fly-posting. As demonstrated in the biomedicalisation chapter (Chapter Three), telemedicine providers such as Women Help Women also collaborate with local organisations to share knowledge and information, and provide extensive on-the-ground training for activists/partners, using a 'train the trainer' model. The telemedicine approach does not reach all those who seek an early abortion; in some circumstances women may use the black market to access medication, herbs or seek the services of unregulated providers.

The results of lack of abortion access can be seen in the two case studies below – the Republic of Ireland and Uruguay – illustrating the slow process of abortion law reform.

Case study: the Republic of Ireland

The Republic of Ireland is situated in the northwest of Europe. It makes up the majority of the island of Ireland, with the northern area forming the separate state of Northern Ireland. The Republic of Ireland was a colony of Britain until 1921. It has a population of 4.6 million, most of whom are Catholic (85%) but with increasing numbers of people identifying as non-religious (Central Statistics Office, 2011). In the latter part of the twentieth century, the country witnessed significant economic growth and was at one stage the sixth richest country in the world. This period of boom was, however, followed by an economic crash, resulting in severe cutbacks in government spending. The recession had a negative impact on employment, housing, education and health. The health system is largely funded by the government, with access categorised into those with a medical card and those without. Access to a medical card is restricted to those on low incomes and who have particular medical conditions. Those with a medical card can access a wide range of health services and medicines free of charge. Those without have limited access to free services and pay reduced costs for all other services (HSE, 2017).

The Republic of Ireland is generally regarded as a conservative society. For most of the twentieth century, the Catholic Church had significant influence over societal norms. Sex was framed as purely for the purpose of procreation; any other purpose was sinful. Contraception was only made available in 1973 (initially only to married women). Divorce was first legalised in 1996 and homosexuality was decriminalised in 1993. The Republic of Ireland has a troubled history on maternal health matters such as single-mother-and-baby homes and Magdalene laundries (homes for orphaned, abandoned girls and women), mass baby graves and symphysiotomy (Bloomer and O'Dowd, 2014; Campbell and Clancy, 2018).

The role of women in society after independence was largely positioned within the home, particularly for those that were married. Women's economic opportunities were limited with the civil service 'marriage bar' (the requirement that women leave paid employment on getting married) (1958–73), which significantly restricted employment opportunities (Bloomer and O'Dowd, 2014). The Irish Constitution (Article 41.2) placed women in the heart of the home in their primary role as mothers: 'by her life within the home, woman gives to the State a support without which the common good cannot be achieved' (Bunreacht na hÉireann 1937: 55). This positioning of women began to change in the late twentieth century due to a combination of factors, including liberalisation of laws on contraception and divorce. However, the state's response to abortion law reform has been both slow and reactionary.

Historically, the legal framework for abortion in the Republic of Ireland was the British Offences Against the Person Act 1861, introduced during colonisation. The act stated that abortion was illegal. Women seeking abortion were left with very limited options. Jackson (1992), in a study of court cases, found that illegal abortion was common among all social classes, with cases of infanticide also noted. The introduction of the Abortion Act 1967 in England provided an opportunity for women from the Republic of Ireland to travel to a nearby country to access safe abortion, though at a cost, with those with restricted travel abilities facing particular barriers. While travelling for abortion or providing information about abortion in England was initially prohibited by the state, a referendum in 1992 resulted in amendments to the Constitution to allow both. The state thus demonstrated an approach of acknowledging the need for abortion, but not within its jurisdiction.

Throughout the latter part of the twentieth century and early twenty-first century, abortion was a highly contentious issue in the Republic of Ireland. Several referendums on the matter were held, resulting in vocal campaigns arguing for and against. One of the most notable, in 1983, resulted in a change to the Constitution allowing the foetus the same rights as the pregnant woman from the moment of conception (known as the 8th Amendment). As de Londras and Enright (2018: 1) explain: 'the moment we become pregnant, our constitutional rights are subordinated to the right to life of the unborn and circumscribed by the constitutional status of "mother".'

Legislation introduced in 2013, the Protection of Life During Pregnancy Act, permits abortions only if the life of the mother is at risk. The legislation has been criticised for being both too limited and overly complicated, requiring the woman to progress through a series of stages in the process of seeking an abortion. The inclusion of the maximum penalty of 14 years' imprisonment for having or assisting in an unlawful abortion was regarded as disproportionate and inconsistent with the state's obligations under international human rights law. In addition, it was argued that the harsh penalty would serve to have a chilling effect on women seeking abortion and health professionals. This was also in the context of significant stigma and silencing in wider society about abortion.

The abortion debate in the Republic of Ireland is marked with a series of significant cases, each of which has highlighted the inadequacies of the law, the prevailing moral conservatism among policy makers and the challenges faced by those implementing the law. The X case, in 1992, involved a 13-year-old girl who became pregnant after rape and travelled to England with her parents to obtain an abortion. Before leaving, the family sought advice from local police on whether DNA testing could be conducted on foetal remains to allow for identification of the rapist. This request came to the attention of the Attorney General who sought an injunction to stop the abortion from being performed. This was later overturned by the Supreme Court on the grounds that the girl was suicidal. The case led to a public debate on the issue of abortion being provided on the grounds of rape. Repeated governments stated they would give the matter due consideration but failed to do so. After over a decade, the Protection of Life During Pregnancy Act was introduced in 2013, allowing abortion in case of suicidal risk. As noted above, it was widely criticised, and as exemplified below, in the case of Miss Y, was found to be unworkable.

In the year preceding the introduction of the Protection of Life During Pregnancy Act, the impact of the 8th Amendment was brought into sharp focus following the death of Savita Halappanavar. In 2012, Ms Halappanavar presented at hospital in Galway exhibiting signs of a miscarriage. She was admitted to hospital where her health deteriorated. She made repeated requests for a termination, but was advised, "This is a Catholic country." Doctors refused to terminate the pregnancy until the foetal heartbeat had stopped. Ms Halappanavar developed complications resulting from septicaemia and later died. Her family assert that her death was avoidable. At her inquest the coroner noted that there had been fear and confusion among medical staff regarding the legality of an abortion being performed.

Two years later, in 2014, a further case highlighted the deep flaws in accessing abortion in the Republic of Ireland. This case centred on a woman known as Miss Y. Miss Y had arrived in the Republic of Ireland in March 2014 as an asylum seeker, and soon after discovered she was pregnant. The pregnancy was as a result of rape that had been committed in her home country. Throughout the period from April to July, Miss Y requested an abortion but was not able to obtain one and was advised that travelling outside of the Republic of Ireland was only possible if she was able to secure travel documentation. During this time delays were experienced in accessing the necessary documentation. The lengthy delays added to the significant stress experienced by Miss Y, with medical staff who assessed her during this time noting that she was 'very distressed' and 'vulnerable' and had a strong 'death wish' (Holland, 2014). At one point in July she attempted to travel to England to obtain an abortion but was arrested, held for 11 hours and refused entry due to incomplete documentation. Upon her return to the Republic of Ireland Miss Y declared to medical staff that she was suicidal, and following admittance to hospital she commenced a hunger strike. In hospital she was hydrated against her will following a court order. Medical staff confirmed she was at risk of suicide should the pregnancy continue. A caesarean section was performed in early August, at approximately 25 weeks' gestation. Following this, Miss Y was discharged from hospital and the infant was placed under the care of the state (Holland, 2014). Miss Y is suing the state and various state bodies, alleging assault, negligence, and reckless and intentional infliction of emotional harm and suffering.

Each of these cases has attracted international media attention and served to galvanise both those who support legal reform and those who oppose it. Typically, opposition to reform is led by the Catholic Church and anti-abortion groups such as the Iona Institute. On the reform side, grassroots feminist group Abortion Rights Campaign began the call for 'Free, safe, legal' in the midst of a fourth wave movement, and the Coalition to Repeal the 8th Amendment coalesced a wide range of political and activist groups to campaign for legal reform. Both groups sought to build on the growing public support for legal reform, which typically stood at 70–80% in public opinion polls. In 2018, in the lead-up to a referendum on the 8th Amendment, these activist groups and the National Women's Council of Ireland came together to form Together For Yes, a national civil society campaign to remove the 8th Amendment. It was an umbrella group, formed for the short time period of the referendum campaign, made up of hundreds of organisations, groups and local community chapters, representing a diverse cross-section of Irish civil society.

The announcement of the referendum had been preceded by a Citizens' Assembly – which had been successfully campaigned for by both the Abortion Rights Campaign and the Coalition to Repeal the 8th Amendment – and a series of hearings by an Oireachtas (government) committee.* These processes involved detailed consideration of a vast amount of evidence, including medical, legal and lived experiences, and resulted in both the Citizens' Assembly and the Oireachtas committee recommending fundamental legal reform. The referendum determined that 66.4% of the population supported reform. This is expected to result in the issuing of a new law, which would allow abortion up to 12 weeks, with additional restrictions placed thereafter. These mechanisms demonstrate how a broad civil base of expert knowledge, combined with the real stories of abortion seekers and their families, helped sway those for whom the issue had previously only ever been an untouchable one.

---

* The Irish government described the Citizens' Assembly as 'an exercise in deliberative democracy, placing the citizen at the heart of important legal and policy issues facing Irish society today. With the benefit of expert, impartial and factual advice the 100 will consider the topics … Their conclusions will form the basis of a number of reports and recommendations that will be submitted to the Houses of the Oireachtas for further debate by our elected representatives.' (https://www.citizensassembly.ie/en). For a critique of this process see: Enright (2017); de Londras and Markicevic (2018).

Statistics on legal abortion are limited in the Republic of Ireland, with a paucity of published sources prior to 2013. Before the introduction of the Protection of Life During Pregnancy Act it was reported during government hearings that abortions performed under legal criteria amounted to an average of 30 per year (Oireachtas, 2013: 55). Statistics released by the state indicate that in 2015 and 2016, 26 abortions per year were carried out under the Protection of Life During Pregnancy Act (Department of Health [Republic of Ireland], 2016). These statistics contrast markedly with the number of women travelling to England for abortion and those travelling elsewhere in Europe. In 2015, for instance, 3,451 women accessing abortions from private providers in England stated that they were resident in the Republic of Ireland. Those travelling to the Netherlands peaked at 461 in 2006, but have since dropped to less than 50 in 2015 (IFPA, 2016). The issue of travel is hugely problematic for those who are asylum seekers and undocumented migrants. These individuals face multiple and complex barriers, including the time, cost and other requirements necessary to access travel visas (Kennedy and Gilmartin, 2018).

Research on the perspective of health professionals in the Republic of Ireland is limited. A recent study by Fitzgerald et al (2014), focusing on medical students, found that despite predominantly pro-choice responses, considerably fewer indicated that they would perform abortions. A recent study of trainee obstetricians in the Republic of Ireland (Aiken et al, 2017a) indicates that travel creates health risks. A scoping study examining healthcare professionals' experiences and perspectives on caregiving for Irish women seeking abortion discovered that illegality and the experience of travel for healthcare created significant issues in quality of care for Irish women (Duffy and Pierson, 2017). These issues include the fact that care structures break down in abortion care, with women immediately referred out of conventional pathways, often to private providers; as such, they may not refer themselves back into the system to access after-care, for example. Restrictive laws also affect interpersonal relationships with care providers. For example, restrictions within the law on information-giving inhibit free and frank discussions on abortion access and services.

Case study: Uruguay

Uruguay is South America's second smallest nation, with a population of 3.42 million people, and is located in the southeastern region between Brazil and Argentina. It is regarded as a high-income country with one of the most stable societies in South America with regard to democracy, peace and a lack of corruption (between 1973 and 1985 the country operated under a military dictatorship). It is a secular country with no official state religion and a significant number of people identifying with no particular church (30%) or as agnostic/atheist (14%). Catholicism is the largest religion, with approximately 45% of the population identifying as Catholic. Uruguay is considered one of the most liberal Latin American countries, being the first to legalise divorce and allow women to vote (Kulczycki, 2011).

Historically, abortion was criminalised in Uruguay under the Penal Code of 1898, except for the period between 1934 and 1938, when abortion was decriminalised due to a public outcry over a woman's death from an unsafe abortion (Wood et al, 2016). Abortion remained a crime until legal reform in 2012, which liberalised the law in certain circumstances. Prior to legalisation, the punishment for having an abortion was 3–12 months in prison, while performing an abortion was punishable by 6–24 months in prison. Judges could apply mitigating factors in sentencing the pregnant woman, including economic hardship, risk to the woman's life, rape or family honour. Public opinion surveys (as shown in the World Values Survey) indicate broad support for abortion law reform (Blofield, 2008). Feminist organisations forged alliances with left-wing feminist politicians in the legislature in the early 2000s, to help put abortion on the political agenda. An additional politicisation of abortion occurred with the arrest of a young woman for obtaining an illegal abortion in 2007, after which over 800 Uruguayans signed a document in solidarity with the woman, admitting to having had an abortion or participated in one.

A movement to liberalise abortion law in 2008 was subsequently vetoed by the president at the time, Tabaré Vázquez, who himself was an obstetrician who opposed abortion. This was despite the fact that the Senate had voted 17 to 13 to support a bill which decriminalised abortion. Subsequently, in 2011, the Senate voted 17 to 14 to support a bill which would decriminalise abortion. The bill allows abortion on request up until 12 weeks and after 12 weeks in cases of rape or incest. The bill was supported by the new president, José Mujica. The new legislation occurred within the context of programmes developed by healthcare professionals to target unsafe abortion, as discussed below.

Despite the change to abortion law, there continue to be challenges with safe abortion access. The new law requires a woman to undergo a consultation with a three-person panel composed of a gynaecologist, psychologist and social worker. The consultation is intended to inform women about the law, alternatives to abortion, and the procedure and its possible risks. However, not all medical facilities have been able to comply with this part of the law: many lack a sufficient number of professionals to form the three-person panel. In 2015, a Uruguayan court ruled in favour of a group of gynaecologists who claimed that the law violates their right to conscientious objection. With high rates of conscientious objection (30% of gynaecologists in Uruguay have exercised conscientious objection), it is obvious that women's access to abortion will be restricted. Statistics show that prior to the reformed law, between 16,000 and 36,000 abortions took place per year. As of January 2014, the Ministry of Public Health reported 420–450 abortions per month. An annual total of 5,040–5,400 abortions were provided within government services, indicating that many women continue to go outside the public health system to access abortion (International Women's Health Coalition, 2014).

Prior to legislative reform, Uruguay had high rates of maternal death due to unsafe abortion (28.7% during the period 1991–2001). A group of healthcare professionals, recognising that decriminalisation would be the best remedy for decreasing maternal death but not having the power to intervene in law, developed a public health programme, Sanitary Initiatives Against Unsafe Abortion (SIAUA), to target unsafe abortion (Briozzo et al, 2006). The obstetricians/gynaecologists also formed an NGO called Iniciativas Sanitarias in 2001, to deliver and manage the programme (the programme has been referred to internationally as the 'Uruguay model').

The programme first ran as a trial in 2004 in the Pereira Rossell Hospital (the main public maternity hospital in the country) and soon after it became an official policy of the Ministry of Health. The programme aimed to provide counselling within the limits of the law to prevent unsafe abortion. It invited women who were uncertain about the status of their pregnancy to a 'before' and 'after' counselling session. Some women self-referred, while others were referred by health professionals. The programme was publicised through a public information campaign. The counselling was intended not to influence the decision of the woman but to provide impartial information about social support, law and the risks involved in the different means used in Uruguay to induce abortion. The 'before' visit also determined that the woman was pregnant and the pregnancy's gestation. The 'after' visit was completely confidential and allowed those who reported having an abortion to have access to a multidisciplinary support team. It also allowed contraception to be provided and uterine aspiration if an incomplete abortion had taken place (Briozzo et al, 2006).

An evaluation of the programme undertaken in 2004 showed a steady increase in women accessing the service, both before and after visits, with around 75% of women who attended the before visit returning for the second visit. Of the 675 women who accessed the service during the evaluation, data was held for 439. Of these women, 88.9% had an induced abortion outside the hospital and

3.5% returned for antenatal care. The other 7.5% were either not pregnant or met the legal requirement for an abortion in the hospital. Those who had induced abortions all used misoprostol. There were no cases of maternal death or severe complications among women participating in the programme or at the hospital at all during the evaluation period (compared with an average of four deaths per year in the preceding three years). There was one case of mild post-abortion infection and two cases of haemorrhage (Briozzo et al, 2006).

A follow-up study conducted in 2015 indicated that maternal mortality had continued to decrease. This decrease is largely ascribed to the harm reduction policy, although it also coincides with a reduction in poverty and an improvement in broader socioeconomic conditions (Briozzo et al, 2016). The programme clearly shows that in situations where abortion is illegal, providing women with information on safe and unsafe methods of abortion and having clear access to post-abortion care can reduce the dangers associated with what are commonly referred to as 'backstreet' abortions.

Why decriminalise?

This chapter has presented examples of the punitive and dangerous effects of restricted abortion access. The argument could be made that the answer is to make exceptions within the criminal law to allow for abortion under particular circumstances. This, we argue, is not the correct approach if we are to achieve social justice for women and excellence in healthcare. What is required is for abortion to be removed from the criminal law entirely and for its governance to be regulated within the rules of medical procedures. In effect, this makes abortion a health procedure, a private matter between a woman and her healthcare provider.

Britain provides a useful example to illustrate the need for decriminalisation. The 1967 Abortion Act provided a number of defences against the 1861 OAPA for doctors, yet outside of these defences it remains a punishable crime under the law. The 1967 act was introduced in the climate of high incidences of 'backstreet' abortions, which were witnessed by healthcare professionals at the time and resulted in death and injury for women. The act allows for abortion under a series of grounds, which broadly permit access in cases of maternal life, health (including mental health), foetal anomaly and socioeconomic status. Further requirements were that abortions could be provided up to 28 weeks, though this was later amended by the Human Fertilisation and Embryology Act 1990 to allow for abortion only up until 24 weeks. The legal framework also states that abortion must be carried out with the consent of two medical practitioners, carried out by a medical practitioner and within a regulated facility.

Statistics from the English Department of Health indicate that the number of women having abortions in England has risen slightly in recent years (by 2.3% from 2016 to 2017, in numerical terms from 185,824 to 189,859). The data also indicates that increasing numbers of women are accessing abortion in their thirties and forties (Department of Health, 2018). The increase in abortion figures and changing demographics have been assigned to difficulties for older women in accessing contraception as a result of cuts to funding of sexual health services, and the fact that these services are viewed as being targeted towards younger people (Campbell, 2016).

Abortion is clearly accessible within the law in Britain, with one in three women having an abortion in her lifetime in the region. However, medical professional bodies, including the Royal College of Obstetricians and Gynaecologists, the Royal College of Midwives and the British Medical Association, have argued that decriminalisation is necessary for a number of reasons.

First, the criminal law is punitive, with prosecution and possible imprisonment of up to 12 years as a result. A number of cases have arisen in the past five years of women procuring their abortion through ordering medication online. One woman, Sarah Catt, took an abortifacient purchased over the internet at over 38 weeks' gestation. She had sought an abortion earlier in her pregnancy but was over the legal time limit. Catt pleaded guilty and was sentenced to eight years' imprisonment. In 2015, a 24-year-old woman pleaded guilty to procuring her own miscarriage at 32–34 weeks pregnant through purchase of abortifacients online. She was sentenced to two and a half years imprisonment (British Medical Association, 2017). In addition, there are a number of cases in Northern Ireland (where the 1967 act does not apply) of women procuring abortifacients online at earlier stages in their pregnancy and being prosecuted for doing so (or for helping another to do so). These prosecutions follow a pattern similar to the criminalisation of certain behaviour during pregnancy. In the US, for instance, the organisation National Advocates for Pregnant Women defends women who have been prosecuted for a range of behaviours, including using alcohol and illegal drugs while pregnant, but also for not following their doctor's orders. The overwhelming majority of those prosecuted in the US are women of colour.

It is argued that the law lags behind medical practice and healthcare advances. The cases noted above concern the use of abortion pills purchased online. For many women, accessing pills to use in their own homes for early stage gestations is both preferable and more affordable than accessing abortion in a clinic setting, avoiding travel and other costs such as childcare. In addition, clinics can often be the site of anti-abortion demonstrations and protests, which can be distressing for women attending clinics and staff.

All healthcare procedures must be regulated, however there are few reasons why early medical abortion must be carried out in a clinic or hospital setting (for miscarriages, the same medication is used and women are often allowed to take it at home). In fact, in 2017 Scotland became the first region of the UK to allow women to take misoprostol home to use when clinically appropriate. In addition, the consent of two practitioners has no clinical reasoning and simply adds burden to the process of the procedure.

Putting abortion within the criminal law also has societal effects. Women in Britain have to construct reasons that fit within the law to justify their abortion to doctors. As such, simply not wanting to be pregnant is not enough; there must be some detriment to physical or mental health, socioeconomic status or to the foetus itself. Having to create narratives which fit within the legal framework continues the stigma associated with abortion (discussed further in Chapter Four). It serves to reinforce the notion of 'good' and 'bad' abortions. This also continues to put the decision in the hands of a doctor rather than the woman herself.

The argument for decriminalisation therefore has several faces: first, to eradicate harsh and unnecessary punishment for abortion; second, to allow for advancements in medicine and healthcare to be taken account of by the law; and third, (and arguably most importantly) to allow women true equality and autonomy in decision-making about their body and pregnancy. It is significant to note that at the time of writing this book there were indications that the UK Parliament would remove sections 58 and 59 of the 1861 OAPA which criminalise abortion. This would be a historic development, with wide ramifications in the UK and beyond.

Conclusions

This chapter has illustrated the impact of criminalising abortion. The reduction of the number of abortions has never resulted from the introduction of criminal penalties, regardless of the intentions of legislators. The impact of restrictive abortion laws is the increase in unsafe, cumbersome or expensive abortion practices, including procurement of an illegal abortion or abortifacients and abortion travel. In addition, criminalisation continues to perpetuate a stigma about abortion as being wrong or against nature, or only justifiable under certain restricted parameters.

As such, it is clear that laws criminalising abortion fail to serve either the purpose of protecting women or preventing abortion. Criminalisation fails to take account of contemporary patient autonomy or modern medical practice or the evolving social morality around abortion in society. Maintaining abortion as a criminal issue places medical professionals and lawyers as gatekeepers to abortion and is unnecessary for medical regulation. It allows women minimal control over their reproductive lives in most settings and completely denies women's autonomy and self-determination in the worst cases.

This chapter provides a basis for arguing that abortion must be taken out of the criminal law, as its inclusion there performs no necessary or proportionate function and serves only to perpetuate archaic and conservative notions towards women and their agency.

THREE

The biomedicalisation of abortion

Introduction

Well before abortion became a regulated healthcare procedure, a range of methods were used by women and lay practitioners to terminate pregnancy. Many of these methods are unsafe and some continue to be used by women where abortion access is restricted.

Grimes et al (2006: 1911) identified almost 50 individual unsafe abortion methods, ranging from ingestion of toxic substances, to inserting of objects or substances into the vagina, and physical pressure on the uterus area. Safe recommended methods, as advocated by the World Health Organization (WHO, 2012), refer to surgical abortion (aspiration, dilution and curettage) and medical abortion. Medical abortion is defined by WHO (2012: iv) as 'the use of pharmacological drugs to terminate pregnancy', while the terms 'non-surgical abortion' or 'medication abortion' are also used in the literature. WHO clinical guidelines advise that medical abortion can be used throughout differing gestations, with regime and clinical requirements changing at each stage (up to 9 weeks, 9–12 weeks, 12–24 weeks, 24 weeks plus) (WHO, 2014). The WHO, in its Safe Abortion Guidelines, states that medical abortion is both safe and effective. Specifically, while alternate medications or combinations of medications are available, it recommends the combined use of mifepristone and misoprostol:

> The most effective regimens rely on the antiprogestogen, mifepristone, which binds to progesterone receptors, inhibiting the action of progesterone and hence interfering with the continuation of pregnancy. Treatment regimens entail an initial dose of mifepristone followed by administration of a synthetic prostaglandin analogue, generally misoprostol, which enhances uterine contractions and aids in expelling the products of conception. (WHO, 2012: 42)

Mifepristone followed by misoprostol for medical abortion has been registered in a range of countries: Austria, Azerbaijan, Belgium,

Finland, France, Georgia, Germany, Greece, India, Israel, Luxembourg, the Netherlands, New Zealand, Norway, the People's Republic of China, Romania, the Russian Federation, South Africa, Spain, Sweden, Switzerland, Tunisia, the UK, Ukraine, the US, Uzbekistan, and Vietnam. However, while the combined use of these medications is included on the complementary WHO 'Model List of Essential Medications', it is of significance that the Director-General of WHO added a note adjacent to the list stating: 'Where permitted under national law and where culturally acceptable' (WHO, 2017a: 46). Inclusion on the full list, without limitations, would result in WHO recommending to all countries that the medications be made available and accessible. As discussed later in the chapter, the story of medical abortion in its development and usage is replete with efforts to restrict it.

The increasing use of medical abortion in the late twentieth and twenty-first centuries can be considered within the broader trend of biomedicalisation, defined by Clarke et al (2009: 384) as 'technical-scientific interventions in biomedical diagnostics, treatments, practices and health, in order to speed more transformations of bodies, the people themselves and their lives'. From a clinical perspective, the initial advantages of abortion medications were that infection risks were reduced, as too were risks of uterine perforations and reactions to anaesthesia (Clarke and Montini, 1993). Most abortion providers were supportive of the biomedicalisation of abortion, and along with those lobbying for improved access to abortion, they welcomed the trend recognising that the medication was easy to administer and inexpensive, transforming abortion care for practitioners, and access for women.

Some, however, were wary of welcoming the trend of the biomedicalisation of abortion, noting that the introduction of the contraceptive pill had been problematic, with women of colour subjected to unethical procedures in trials (Charo, 1991; Raymond et al, 1991; Clarke and Montini, 1993). Specifically, reproductive justice advocates in the US were concerned that the medications had not been sufficiently tested on women of colour; nor had their likelihood to attend follow-up care been considered (Silliman et al, 2016: 19). There was also criticism that the biomedicalisation trend was essentially patriarchal: that the biomedical framework atomised women's body and adopted a utilitarian approach to reproductive capacities. Largely, however, the trend towards biomedicalisation was welcomed, with the majority of feminist groups and women's health organisations agreeing that women should benefit from advances in science and technology.

This chapter will chart the history of the biomedicalisation of abortion and trends in usage in restricted and unrestricted settings. We will focus on the two main types of medication, mifepristone and misoprostol, both of which entered usage in the latter part of the twentieth century. The chapter will also consider how the introduction of the biomedicalisation of abortion impacted on the role of health professionals, and will unpack how bringing health advancements in abortion care sits with a feminist approach to women's health.

The history of the biomedicalisation of abortion

Mifepristone

Mifepristone, also known as RU 486, was developed in France during the 1970s, with testing by the pharmaceutical company Roussel Uclaf beginning in the early 1980s. This testing sought to develop medication that would act as an anti-hormone, blocking receptors to prevent the uterus from retaining the fertilised egg, thereby inducing an abortion. Dr Etienne-Emile Baulieu, from France's National Institute of Health and Medical Research, is the name primarily associated with the development of mifepristone. The literature is dominated by the role he played, with support from company president Edouard Sakiz. However, it was Roussel Uclaf scientists Teutsch and Philibert who led the team that worked on the compound and it is they who are named on the patent. As a special advisor to Roussel Uclaf, Baulieu worked with colleagues to test the formula. By the time it was released for wider use in 1988, it had been trialled on over 7,000 women in France and 3,000 in China, as well as smaller numbers in Sweden, the US, England and Scotland (Greenhouse, 1989; Charo, 1991; Lader, 1991). In parallel with the testing, Baulieu played a highly significant role in promoting mifepristone, both within France and across the globe. His persuasive communication skills soon led to him being positioned as a brand ambassador, much to the consternation of colleagues, including Teutsch (Lader, 1991). It is noteworthy that absent in much of the literature about the mifepristone story was the role played by women, such as Catherine Euvrard, Director of Communications and Scientific Relations at Roussel Uclaf, who worked closely with Baulieu to promote the use of mifepristone. Baulieu and Euvrard also worked with a team of doctors, including Elizabeth Aubeny and Annie Bureau-Rogers, who trialled the medication in hospital settings, provided tours to visiting medics and travelled internationally to promote the medication (Jackman, 2002).

The silencing of women's role in important scientific discoveries is not exclusive to the mifepristone story.

Though the introduction of mifepristone was welcomed by many as a safer and more cost-effective alternative to surgical methods of abortion, it was also subject to significant attention from anti-abortionists. The controversy when the medication first emerged mirrored that associated with the introduction of the contraceptive pill. Arguments about its use, largely centring morality issues, resulted in the contraceptive pill being initially marketed as a method of menstrual regulation rather than for its main purpose (Eig, 2016). When news of the development of mifepristone was announced, a vigorous and sustained campaign by anti-abortionists was launched in France and in countries considering its introduction. In the US, for instance, Charo (1991: 45) notes that not only would Roussel Uclaf have to contend with obtaining approval from the Food and Drug Administration, at a cost of $50 million, but such costs had to be weighed against dealing with a strong anti-abortion lobby. The activities of such organisations were labelled as 'industrial terrorism' by one commentator (Segal, cited in Clarke and Montini, 1993: 51). This 'industrial terrorism' comprised a sustained campaign against mifepristone, boycotting products from high-profile French companies such as Perrier and Michelin tyres (in the US), threats to boycott all products from Roussel Uclaf (in the US), threats to pharmaceutical company employees and their families, and public protests at the company's AGM (France). Anti-abortionists claimed that mifepristone was a chemical weapon and that it trivialised abortion (Charo, 1991: 61, 47). They also argued that it would lead to genocide in developing countries; though notably these anti-abortion campaigns offered little to counteract high levels of maternal mortality in the same countries (Charo, 1991: 71). In contrast, in the US counter-boycotts were threatened against Roussel Uclaf's parent company Hoechst AG, if it withdrew support for allowing the medication to be licensed (Jackman, 2002).

The scientists leading the development of mifepristone not only had to contend with external pressures from the anti-abortion movement, but encountered hostility within their own company. Hoechst AG distanced itself from the product, with the company's chief executive officer, Wolfgang Hilger, stating that the medication violated the company's ethos to support life (Greenhouse, 1989).

The autumn of 1988 witnessed a remarkable development in the mifepristone debate. On 23 September 1988, the French government approved the medication for use as an abortifacient. The resulting controversy, including very public criticism from Catholic bishops, led to further pressure on Roussel Uclaf. At an internal company meeting one month later, the potential of a lengthy boycott of all products, the lack of high profit margins, the impact on staff of hostile campaigns and the efforts of management in defending the product led to a decision to withdraw the medication (Greenhouse, 1989). The announcement occurred at the same time that almost 10,000 health professionals were attending the World Congress of Gynecology and Obstetrics in Brazil. When news of the decision reached delegates, the focus of the conference shifted to the status of mifepristone in France. The outcry at the decision, combined with support from family planning organisations and feminist groups, formed a large supportive voice calling for the medication to be reinstated. In parallel, the French government was also unhappy at the decision. The health minister Claude Evin argued that mifepristone had become the moral property of women and that they should not be deprived of it. There was also concern that withdrawing the medication would not only reduce access but could be interpreted as encouragement for the anti-abortion lobby to move against abortion access more widely, for example, by seeking to revise abortion legislation (Greenhouse, 1989). Within two days, the French government ordered the company to reverse its decision or risk losing its patent to a rival. This clear demonstration of support from the government provided Roussel Uclaf with a defence to reverse their decision and mifepristone was released back to the market (Greenhouse, 1989; Charo, 1991). Roussel Uclaf president, Sakiz, would later claim that the temporary withdrawal of the medication had allowed the health minister to gather political support (Lader, 1991: 51). Rumours also circulated that the temporary withdrawal of the medication had been orchestrated as a ploy to gain public support and minimise criticism of the company.

Once the initial controversy abated, mifepristone became commonly used in France, and in China, which also had a licence for the medication. However, its use elsewhere was subject to numerous delays. Intimidation from the anti-abortion movement resulted in corporate pressure within companies and subsidiaries, leading to them proceeding with caution. In later years, companies operating in one country would refuse to sell it in another country, citing vague reasons such as incompatibility with the company's objectives or the absence of technical guarantees (Charo, 1991: 75). To overcome corporate pressures, new pharmaceutical companies emerged, focused solely on mifepristone.

Mifepristone is currently registered/approved for use in almost 60 countries (see Table 1 below). Lader (1991: 66) argues that the initial distribution of mifepristone by Roussel Uclaf followed a pattern of elitism, determined by convenience rather than need. For Lader, company motivations were not primarily based on reducing unsafe abortion in developing countries, but on promoting the medication in countries where access was relatively easy. Typically, this included a focus on the Global North, in countries with high Protestant populations, reducing the risk of encountering extreme opposition. As a company motivated by commercial priorities, the path of least resistance adopted by Roussel Uclaf is unsurprising. Making the medication available in countries where hostility was evident, and/or health infrastructure was underdeveloped, would have made distribution more difficult and cost the company financially.

Table 1: Countries where mifepristone is registered/licensed

Year	Country
1988	China, France
1991	UK
1992	Sweden
1999	Austria, Belgium, Denmark, Finland, Germany, Greece, Israel, Luxembourg, Netherlands, Spain, Switzerland
2000	Norway, Taiwan, Tunisia, US
2001	New Zealand, South Africa, Ukraine
2002	Belarus, Georgia, India, Latvia, Russia, Serbia, Vietnam
2003	Estonia
2004	Guyana, Moldova
2005	Albania, Hungary, Mongolia, Uzbekistan
2006	Kazakhstan
2007	Armenia, Kyrgyzstan, Portugal, Tajikistan
2008	Romania, Nepal
2009	Italy, Cambodia
2010	Zambia
2011	Ghana, Mexico, Mozambique
2012	Australia, Ethiopia, Kenya
2013	Azerbaijan, Bangladesh, Bulgaria, Czech Republic, Slovenia, Uganda, Uruguay
2014	Thailand
2015	Canada
2017	Colombia

Source: http://gynuity.org/downloads/resources/biblio_ref_lst__mife.pdf

In terms of which settings the medication would be used in, the early literature on mifepristone assumed that it would be used in medical practices, not limited to abortion clinics, thus providing both the woman and doctor with anonymity (Lader, 1991; Jackman, 2002). Such expectations were evidenced in the debate on mifepristone in the US. During a lengthy campaign over six years, feminist groups, medical groups and other interested parties lobbied for the drug's introduction without the burden of numerous restrictions (Clarke and Montini, 1993; Jackman, 2002). However, regulations in many states limited abortion medication to abortion providers in clinical settings even at early gestations of less than nine weeks. Notably, as discussed later in this chapter, today there is a growing trend for medical abortion at home, away from clinical settings, for early gestation stages.

Misoprostol

The medication misoprostol was primarily developed for the prevention and treatment of gastroduodenal ulcers. Introduced in 1985, it soon become available, often without prescription, in over 80 countries under the brand name Cytotec. As with mifepristone, the medication is relatively inexpensive to produce and store, easy to administer and has limited side effects (Weeks et al, 2005). The use of misoprostol as an abortifacient was first reported in medical journals in the early 1990s as a method of obtaining illegal abortions, primarily in Brazil (see the case study later in this chapter). Its use as an abortifacient in Brazil was set against a context of poor access to contraception, high numbers of unwanted pregnancies, unsafe abortions and a highly restrictive abortion law (Costa and Vessey, 1993). Knowledge of misoprostol's property as an abortifacient was shared through informal networks in communities, with medics noting its increasing use as women presented at hospitals after having taken the medication. Later studies documented further applications, such as in the treatment for partial miscarriages/spontaneous abortions, induction of labour and as treatment for postpartum haemorrhaging (Weeks et al, 2005). Knowledge of misoprostol's use spread to other Latin American countries and to Europe and beyond via Latin American migrants (de Zordo, 2016).

Remarkably, despite repeated studies demonstrating its effectiveness and safety, the drug manufacturer Searle (later part of Pfizer), has been reluctant to seek a license for reproductive uses. As with mifepristone in the US, this decision was partly related to the economics of obtaining a license: the average cost was estimated at $897 million in the latter part of the twentieth century (Weeks et al, 2005). The absence of a license did not prevent the medication being listed in the US as part of an abortion regimen with misoprostol. Indeed, this absence was not a barrier to the medication being listed as an abortifacient in many countries around the world (see Figure 1). Common usage in the absence of a license is not unique to abortion medication. However, intertwined with cost considerations is the view that the anti–abortion lobby was also influential with regard to licensing. The pharmaceutical company could justifiably sidestep the abortion debate by confirming that the medication's intended use was not as an abortifacient, and thus avoid the boycotting associated with mifepristone. In return, despite not playing an active role in promoting its use as an abortifacient, Searle benefits from increased sales (de Zordo, 2016).

In countries where access to abortion is highly restricted, for example, the Philippines, developments regarding abortion medication were regarded with hostility by governments. The use of misoprostol was challenged under Philippines law, which states that abortifacients must be banned even if the drug may be indicated for other medical conditions. In 2002 the Philippines Bureau of Food and Drugs (BFAD) stated that regarding 'the unregistered drug product known as misoprostol (Cytotec) … manufacture, importation, exportation, sale, offering for sale distribution, of transfer of … is considered a violation of R.A. 3720 as amended otherwise known as the "Food, Drugs, Devices and Cosmetics Act"' (FDA, 2002: 1).

Hostility to the abortifacient effects of misoprostol today is evidenced either by non-certification by food and drug authorities or the withdrawal of initial certifications. The use of misoprostol is now limited to hospitals in countries such as Brazil and Egypt, for instance, where it was once widely available at pharmacies.

The availability of abortion medication in restricted settings

In the face of government hostility to abortion, the biomedicalisation of abortion provided an opportunity to improve access to safe abortion in countries where access was problematic due to legal or other restrictions, as discussed in the previous chapter. Organisations operating nationally and internationally recognised that abortion medication could be offered outside official settings in order to circumvent barriers. One such organisation, Women on Waves, had originally been established to provide surgical abortions on board a ship that travelled to countries where abortion was inaccessible. Upon

Figure 1: Global map of countries where misoprostol is approved

Misoprostol Approved

approved

not approved

© 2017 Gynuity Health Projects
Updated December 2017

Gynuity Health Projects tracks formal drug registration and government approval of misoprostol throughout the world. This map reflects our latest information. If you become aware of registration or approval in new countries, please write to pubinfo@gynuity.org

Source: http://gynuity.org/resources/single/map-of-misoprostol-approvals/

development of abortion medication, Women on Waves developed its programme to include medical abortions for early gestation stages. Using the internet as a means of promoting access, Women on Waves established Women on Web (WOW), a digital collective of women who have had abortions, medical doctors, researchers, and individuals and organisations that support abortion rights. As outlined in Chapter Two, it operates digitally, on a multilingual basis, to provide information on abortion medication. It provides abortion medication to those who meet set criteria and have completed an online consultation with a doctor.

Organisations such as Safe2Choose, WOW and Women Help Women (discussed in Chapter Six) typically provide a combination of misoprostol and mifepristone medication, in line with WHO (2012) recommendations. However, it is also recognised that while the combination of mifepristone and misoprostol is most effective (in 98% of cases), misoprostol can also be used on its own, though its effectiveness is less (84%). WHO guidelines for safe abortion provide protocols for the use of misoprostol alone, recognising that it is more easily available in some settings. The use of misoprostol on its own clearly presents ethical issues, as it is not as effective as when it is used with mifepristone.

The fact that many seeking abortions must make do with less than the 'gold standard' of care is problematic. Furthermore, evidence suggests that in restricted settings there is often a dearth of up-to-date information about safety, effectiveness and appropriate regimens (Sherris et al, 2005). By implication, health risks could be increased if medications are being used ineffectively, as discussed in the following section. Counteracting this, organisations offering abortion medication in restricted settings typically conduct follow-up assessments for those who have used abortion medication. Organisations including WOW and Women Help Women also provide advice to local activists on protocols for the use of abortion medication, and advice on avoiding detection by medical and state authorities should the woman need to seek post-abortion care. Emphasis is placed on symptoms being the same as that of a miscarriage/spontaneous abortion, and the fact that the medication cannot be traced if a woman presents herself at a medical clinic/hospital. Women Help Women, for instance, provides extensive on-the-ground training for activists/partners, using a 'train the trainer' model. Its website also provides full protocols in several languages for use of misoprostol alone (as well as for mifepristone and misoprostol together). The model further provides additional support for local hotlines. Women Help Women asserts that misoprostol alone is a better choice for those in restricted settings where customs regulations or inefficient postal systems make telemedicine an impractical solution (interview with Women Help Women, 2017). Online providers typically advocate the use of the medication up to nine weeks' gestation, for those seeking abortion away from clinical settings, yet there is growing evidence of the safety of its use in the 12–24 weeks' gestation stages (Zurbriggen et al, 2017).

Abortion information hotlines have been set up in at least 20 countries where abortion is restricted. Drawing on networks of activist groups and a range of communication methods, these organisations provide manuals, leaflets and videos about abortion medication, explaining how it can be used safely and how to seek help if it is needed. The hotlines aim to provide information about unwanted pregnancy, abortion and post-abortion care, with some also providing information about contraception and emergency contraception (International Campaign for Women's Right to Safe Abortion, 2017a). Away from restricted settings, evidence suggests that abortion medication is being accessed by women without prescription. In Armenia, a former Soviet Union country, research suggests that women are self-medicating for a range of reasons, including financial considerations. The cost of misoprostol is equivalent to $2.50, which contrasts with $25.00 for an abortion in a hospital setting (Jilozian and Agadjanian, 2016). Other reasons for seeking abortion medication in countries where abortion is typically easy to access include delays in getting referrals from primary healthcare providers, practical barriers related to having to travel to an abortion provider, privacy concerns, lack of eligibility for free services and movements being restricted due to partner/family control (Aiken et al, 2017c).

Abortion medication in restricted settings: risks

In restricted settings the information available on abortion medication can impact on its usage, and access to follow-up care will likely be affected. Studies indicate that in restricted settings abortion medication is typically available via three sources: local pharmacies, the black market and internet-based providers. Additional sources for misoprostol include internet veterinary supply stores and veterinarians, as it is used to treat ulcers and arthritis in dogs, and over the counter in Mexico and many other Latin American countries, where it is sold as Cyrux and Cytotec (Women Help Women, 2017). Jilozian and Agadjanian, (2016) note that self-prescription, away from regulated settings, brings with it additional risks; for example, incorrect dosages may be administered and follow-up care may not be sought. The situation may lead to lack of disclosure and result in a lack of support (Sheldon, 2016). The fact that those accessing abortion medication are often under threat of criminality presents an added stressful dimension.

Zamberlin et al (2012), in a review of multiple South American studies, found that women seeking medical abortion outside of clinic supervision were often fearful of negative consequences to their health as well as being anxious about having acted in a clandestine manner. The authors note that 'the presence of significant others and social networks are helpful during the whole process' (Zamberlin et al, 2012: 8).

In unregulated settings, a study of pharmacy provision of medical abortifacients in a large, unidentified, Latin American city, found that ineffective or potentially dangerous medications were offered as abortifacients (Lara et al, 2006). The study determined that misoprostol was offered by 60% of pharmacy staff approached for advice on abortion medication. However, information on its use was often incomplete and of poor quality, and failed to include sufficient information on adequate dosage, route of administration, side effects, complications and effectiveness. Such findings are replicated in other countries, including those where abortion is legal, for example, Bangladesh (Huda et al, 2014), Zambia (Hendrickson et al, 2016), India (Powell-Jackson et al, 2015) and Kenya (Reiss et al, 2016).

The use of telemedicine online has facilitated access to safer abortion medication for women in restricted settings, yet there will always be safety issues in an online extra-legal setting. The internet allows access to multiple sites where one can order misoprostol and mifepristone. A Google search for the term 'abortion pill' at the time of writing this book resulted in 3.42 million hits. The proliferation of information sources and those selling medication presents risks, as some providers are unreliable, either taking a payment and not sending any medication or sending fake tablets which will not have the desired effect. The extent of fake medication is unknown, though the Women on Web website lists 154 sites that women are advised to avoid (Women on Web, 2017). The Samsara website lists 45 providers to be avoided for Indonesia alone (it also lists a small number of safe providers) (Samsara, 2017). Marge Berer, of the International Campaign for Women's Right to Safe Abortion (ICWRSA), has expressed concern that there are many scam providers, noting that "they appear to spring up and disappear in many places, so it is difficult to count or pin them down, and therefore anyone seeking pills needs to be sure they are getting them from a bona fide source" (interview with Marge Berer, ICWRSA,

2018). As an example of this, Berer highlights reports of 'criminal herbalists' operating in the Philippines who provide a range of herbs to induce abortion, and offer a pill labelled 'Cytotec' for second trimester abortions (Winn, 2017).

Despite recent studies showing that abortion medication accessed from online providers is typically safe (Murtagh et al, 2017), valid concerns remain over unscrupulous providers. Additionally, navigating internet-based information requires the person conducting the search to have sufficient knowledge to allow them to be discerning. This mode of accessing abortion medication is also only available to those have access to the internet and the capacity to pay. Thus, telemedicine approaches are only suitable for some demographics.

The impact of biomedicalisation

The biomedicalisation of abortion was hailed as a significant development in the efforts to reduce abortion mortality. To evidence this, quantification of the usage of abortion medication is required. Official statistics indicate that uptake of medical abortion is variable in settings where it is permitted. In Sweden medical abortion accounts for 91% of all abortions (National Board of Health and Welfare, 2016). In Tunisia 70% of women choose medical abortion (Hajri et al, 2004). In England and Wales medical abortion accounts for 65% of all abortions, a figure that has steadily increased since medication was first introduced in 1991, when it then accounted for 4% of abortions (Department of Health, 2018). In the US 22% of abortions are carried out using medication (Jatlaoui et al, 2016). Although levels remain lower than expected, since medical abortion was introduced in 2000, it has been used by more than 2.75 million women in the United States (Danco, 2016).

Offering a comprehensive analysis of the global usage and impact of abortion medication is challenging due to a multitude of issues, including how data is collected, how abortions are recorded, and the reluctance of women and abortion providers to report usage in settings where access is restricted. As noted in previous sections, further complications arise due to the position of pharmaceutical companies and licencing/regulations, which in the case of misoprostol have led to an avoidance of stating its purpose as an abortifacient, thus making data on sales of the medication problematic. Researchers have sought to overcome these challenges, positing a combination of methods to measure usage and impact. Methods include analysing hospital records of abortion complications, analysing national pharmacy sales data sets, conducting primary research (typically surveys or face-to-face interviews) with women and providers, and pharmacy-based 'mystery client' studies. The listed sources of data have their limitations but each offers a perspective on the quantity and impact of abortion medication, either single use of each type or combined (Wilson et al, 2010: 191).

Specifically, in terms of assessing the impact of abortion medication, interrogation of national data on facility-based treatment of abortion complications can provide an overview of temporal trends. A study by Singh et al (2012: 99), which analysed data in Brazil from 1992 to 2009, observed that there had been a notable decrease (41%) in the number and rate of women being treated for abortion complications. The authors concluded that this was likely to be related to the greater availability of safer abortion methods, increased ability to pay for such methods and more widespread use of modern contraception (the case study that follows discusses this further). Smaller-scale studies in specific regions such as the Dominican Republic also provide evidence of the health benefits of misoprostol only, with complications falling from 11.7% to 1.7% (Miller et al, 2005).

Studies using statistical modelling techniques also offer alternative methods of assessing the impact of abortion medication. Estimates indicate that in restricted settings, such as those in South America, if misoprostol alone was used, mortality rates could decrease by 26%. This was based on calculations of 40% of abortions being misoprostol-induced. In Africa and Asia, the estimated decrease would be 33% and 30% respectively (Harper et al, 2007).

Case study: Brazil

Brazil is the largest country in South America, with a population of 210.7 million.[*] The country is divided into five main regions, each with its own individual economic, cultural and demographic profile. A consideration of rural/urban areas reveals notable differences: while 93% of the urban population have access to adequate-quality drinking water, only 31.5% of the rural population have similar access. Those living in rural areas also contend with environmental challenges such as landslides (most as a consequence of deforestation and road building), high rates of air pollution and pesticide poisoning – all factors which impact significantly on the health and quality of life of rural populations (Pan American Health Organization, 2017). The poorest regions are in the north and northeast and are mostly rural areas. These regions have the lowest levels of development and have fertility rates higher than the rest of the country.

---

[*]   www.worldometers.info/world-population/brazil-population/

In the latter part of the twentieth century, Brazil experienced significant economic growth. While there were improvements in health and socioeconomic indicators (for example, child mortality, maternal mortality and literacy levels), income inequality became more pronounced, favouring those in higher income bands (Medeiros et al, 2015). Significant levels of deprivation remain, with 21% of the population living in poverty. Health inequalities are evident between the affluent and poor; and between black, white and indigenous populations; urban and rural areas; and men and women.

Health services in Brazil are provided free by the state through the Unified Health System (UHS). The infrastructure of the UHS comprises 6,000 hospitals and more than 60,000 outpatient centres. The affluent make use of private health services (estimated at 25% of the population) (Pan American Health Organization, 2017). This two-tiered system has exacerbated health inequalities between the rich and the poor, as the UHS is regarded as stretched in terms of resources and unable to meet the needs of the population as a whole.

More broadly, although Brazilian society is not regarded as particularly morally conservative, in terms of legislation, progress has been slow on tackling social justice issues, including those with a gender focus. This is exemplified by repeated attempts to restrict gender and sexuality education in schools. The slow pace of change is attributed to several factors, including the absence of an effective progressive women's caucus in parliament, the dominance of presidential power, and the role that the Catholic and ultraconservative evangelical organisations play in influencing policymaking (Htun and Power, 2006; Gianella et al, 2017; interview with Marisa Viana, RESURJ, 2018).

Access to abortion in Brazil

During the latter part of the twentieth century and beginning of the twenty-first century maternal mortality in Brazil decreased from 104 per 100,000 live births (in 1990) to 44 per 100,000 live births in 2015 (WHO, 2016). This improvement is ascribed to factors including a reduction in income disparities, improved access to education and decreased fertility rates (Victora et al, 2011). Caution is urged, however, in considering the statistics, as rates have not been adjusted for improved detection and reporting of maternal deaths, which were previously overlooked by the vital registration system (RESURJ et al, 2015a: 8). In parallel, the conservative approach to reproductive health is evident in relation to access to abortion, which is governed by a legal framework under the criminal code that since 2012 has allowed abortion only in cases of risk to the life of the woman, rape or in instances of anencephaly. As a result, a considerable disparity exists between the number of legal and illegal abortions. Official data from 2013 indicates that 1,520 legal abortions were carried out within the UHS, in contrast to the estimated 500,000 illegal abortions carried out annually (Bowater, 2015; Diniz et al, 2017).

Safe, illegal, abortions are carried out within the private sector, though the cost is prohibitive for those on lower incomes, who instead use of range of methods to terminate a pregnancy, including herbal teas, insertion of objects or poison into the uterus, and force exerted on the uterus. These methods bring with them considerable risk, and can result in complications such as haemorrhaging or infection and ultimately hospitalisation. Misoprostol provides the safest method for obtaining an illegal abortion (de Zordo, 2016). As noted earlier, misoprostol first emerged in Brazil as an abortifacient under the brand name of Cytotec during the late 1980s and early 1990s, when informal networks spread news that it could be used beyond its primary purpose as a treatment for gastric ulcers. While reliable data on its usage is problematic due to black market sales, research with women and health providers indicates that it is the most common method of abortion in Brazil (Costa and Vessey, 1993; Martins-Melo et al, 2014).

The conservative approach to abortion in Brazil affects abortion care. Women presenting at hospitals in Brazil with post-abortion complications encounter a range of responses from health providers. Studies indicate that while some receive support, others experience delays and neglect in treatment, an absence of post-abortion contraceptive information, being threatened with prison, and verbal abuse (Victora et al, 2011; Diniz et al, 2012; de Zordo, 2016). De Zordo's (2016) research in the Brazilian state of Bahia reveals a largely conservative position on abortion exhibited by medical staff, ranging from views that women were using misoprostol too readily as a contraceptive, through to blatant hostility. As an example, one doctor described how, if a woman presented with miscarriage symptoms stating she had sustained a fright which caused the miscarriage, he would ask them "if they had fallen on a box of Cytotec" (de Zordo, 2016: 29). Another more extreme position was to delay treatment as a punishment: "they must 'suffer' the pain" (de Zordo, 2016: 29). Most doctors stated they would involve police in extreme cases, such as the death of the women or if the termination had been at a late stage and foetal remains were absent. Doctors expressed concern that they had observed cases where misoprostol had been taken in excessively high dosages and/or at advanced stages of gestation (de Zordo, 2016: 29). Evident within the views of the doctors were issues of class: wealthy clients were viewed as responsible, the poor as irresponsible. The stigmatisation of abortion was also prevalent in these views.

The Zika virus and Brazil

The limited access to abortion was brought into sharp focus in the autumn of 2015 when the Brazilian Ministry of Health announced that there had been an unusual increase in cases of microcephaly (a severe neurological disorder which affects the foetal development of the brain and skull and contributes to developmental problems). It was reported that 141 cases of microcephaly had been detected in the northeast of Brazil within the previous 11 months, by far exceeding the average of 10 cases per year (Pan American Health Organization, 2015).

In February 2016, the World Health Organization declared the matter a public health emergency of international concern. The rise in cases of microcephaly was later ascribed to the Zika virus, which is commonly spread through the *Aedes aegypti* species of mosquitos. Viana and Gumieri (2016: 1) note that while much of the focus on the Zika virus concentrated on microcephaly, within the epidemic microcephaly is only the first sign of a new condition referred to as congenital Zika syndrome, which may include other severe malformations. The virus has no known cure or readily available vaccine, and thus its increased incidence presented unprecedented health risks to the population. The virus spread rapidly, with an estimated 1.5 million cases in Brazil in 2016. The WHO estimated that potentially 4 million people in the Americas were affected (Hodge et al, 2016). The government in Brazil and other countries attempted to control the spread of the virus and issued health warnings, including the extraordinary warning that women should avoid pregnancy for months, years or even indefinitely. Hodge et al (2016: 1) point out that such advice was not only unproven, but that the legality and ethics were highly suspect, noting that in 'many of these countries, women experience significant rates of sexual violence. Their access to contraceptives or abortions to terminate at-risk pregnancies due to Zika virus is legally restricted or practically unavailable'. Asking women to avoid pregnancy was in fact an almost impossible ask.

As a response to this dire situation, Women on Web offered to provide the medication free to women in affected areas. Data from their helpline reveals a significant increase in requests from baseline levels (pre-Zika crisis), from 36% to 108% (Aiken et al, 2016). Women Help Women notes that getting abortion medication into affected areas of Brazil has been problematic. Consequently, the organisation focused its efforts on working with locally based organisations to share information about reliable sources of medicines and accurate information about Zika risks (interview with Women Help Women, 2017). Feminist reproductive health organisations also refocused their campaigns, calling for rapid legal changes that would expand access to legal and safe abortion in the emergency crisis brought about by the Zika virus. In Brazil, a trend in court rulings indicated that legal reform was possible. In a landmark court case in December 2016 a judge ruled that abortions were not illegal in the first trimester and that the criminal abortion laws violate women's fundamental rights. The ruling did not change the law but rather served as a symbolic act demonstrating that legal change was possible (Galli, 2016). Less than 12 months later, in 2017, a setback occurred when a proposed constitutional amendment to recognise life from conception was approved in the Chamber of Deputies (the lower house of the National Congress). The amendment could be interpreted as a ban on all cases where abortion is legal in Brazil: rape, risk to the woman's life and anencephaly. This creates legal insecurity, for while it does not change abortion provisions specifically, the criminal code has to be interpreted according to the Constitution, and thus it paves the way for further criminalisation (interview with Marisa Viana, RESURJ, 2018).

The role of health professionals in biomedicalisation

The introduction of medication for abortifacient purposes was highly symbolic in changing the dynamic of the relationship between clinicians and women seeking abortions. The woman, by being responsible for ingesting/inserting the medication, effectively became the one who was 'performing' the abortion. The clinician has largely remained in control of prescribing the medication, offering counselling, and preliminary and follow-up examinations (Joffe et al, 2004). Early studies on clinicians' views of biomedicalisation of abortion reveal that women seeking medical abortion were positioned as being more 'empowered' than those having surgical abortion, and that the clinician was losing power over their patients' abortion experiences (Simonds et al, 2001: 207). Paternalistic values exhibited by clinicians can clash with the autonomy provided by abortion medication. In practical terms, the use of medication also presents some challenges to clinicians. Surgical methods can be assessed on effectiveness immediately, and the timing of the process is also managed in accordance with clinical times – these are all within the control of clinicians. "This loss of control can be problematic for some clinicians, their role changes from being hands-on to an information provider, but usually when presented with the benefits for the woman of self-managed abortion, they can take a step back and see it from a different perspective" (interview with Women Help Women, 2017).

In terms of clinical management, two trends have emerged in the last decade. First, the role of other clinicians, such as nurses, midwives, pharmacists and health support staff, has become more salient in medical abortion provision (Warriner et al, 2011; Purcell et al, 2017; Tamang et al, 2017). Second, early gestation abortions carried out at home, away from clinical settings, have become more common in both unrestricted and restricted settings. Several studies provide clear evidence of the effectiveness of this approach. Ngo et al (2011), in a systematic review of nine studies comprising 4,522 participants, observed that, in terms of setting, home-based abortion is safe, and there is no difference in effectiveness or acceptability between home-based and clinic-based medical abortion across countries. Similar results were observed in a study comprising 8,765 telemedicine and 10,405 in-person medical abortions (Grossman and Grindlay, 2017).

Gold and Chong (2015) argue that abortion away from clinical settings remains problematic despite repeated evidence that medication is safe. This is impacted by a range of factors in the US, which are mirrored more broadly, including the following:

- Health professionals still view abortion as risky and believe that women undertaking medical abortion should be supervised.
- Some view medical abortion as a procedure, as opposed to a treatment which can be administered away from supervision.
- The absence of clear clinical guidelines leads to misunderstanding as to the mechanisms for distribution of and dispensing the medication.
- Finally, the ongoing contentious nature of the abortion debate in the US makes providers 'reluctant to do anything that seems remotely out of the ordinary'. (Gold and Chong, 2015: 195)

It is expected that the growing body of evidence demonstrating the safety and effectiveness of the medication will help circumvent some of these barriers. However, it is important to recognise that, as previously discussed, those accessing abortion medication in restricted settings still contend with issues related to the quality of the medication, misinformation and an absence of support. Aftercare in such settings is also problematic.

Conclusion

As demonstrated in this chapter, the biomedicalisation of abortion presents as a typical example of the fact that technology can be politicised. Specifically, the evidence demonstrates that the use of abortion medication can be subject to political framing by the state. It has also been subject to limitations arising from the commercial ethos of the pharmaceutical industry. In reflecting on the history of mifepristone, it is evident that while individuals such as Catherine Euvrard and

Etienne-Emile Baulieu fought within the industry, alongside health and feminist organisations, to promote use of abortion medication, the licencing of abortion medication was constrained by concerns about the impact of anti-abortion campaigns. Commercial pressures often outweighed the need to provide improved access to abortion.

In contrast to the pharmaceutical industry-led development of mifepristone, the story of misoprostol is dominated by the nameless women who first identified its abortifacient properties. Knowledge of its effectiveness spread through local, national and international networks. Those advocating its use did so in a context of highly restricted access to abortion, poor socioeconomic conditions and high levels of maternal mortality. Women took power into their own hands. They did so at great risk, not only of criminality, but also of encountering stigma and hostility from health professionals should they need aftercare. In contrast, Searle/Pfizer, as the manufacturer of misoprostol, has largely sidestepped the risk, benefiting from increased sales, but not shouldering any of the responsibility.

Local, national and transnational feminist and health organisations have stepped into the void created by legal restrictions and provided access to abortion medication. Their aim is to provide safe access to abortion, following guidelines from the WHO. In some settings, providing the 'gold standard' is not always possible. Such situations present organisations with ethical challenges, for instance, when the combination of misoprostol and mifepristone medication is not available, and women only have access to misoprostol. As discussed in Chapter Six on activism, these organisations establish partnerships with local organisations to increase awareness and improve effectiveness of the medication, with organisations such as Women Help Women arguing that self-managed abortion is not less than the 'gold standard'. Evident within this debate on standards is that the global women's health movement is not unanimous on this point.

The benefits of abortion medication, in terms of allowing women greater autonomy over the abortion process, have been limited by overregulation and a paternalistic approach to healthcare. Abortion medication has resulted in changes to the dynamics of the relationship between clinicians and those seeking abortions. More fundamentally, particularly where abortion is restricted, it has provided a means to circumvent restrictions, allowing women to self-abort at home and away from regulated settings. Increased use of abortion medication has impacted positively on maternal mortality, however issues of aftercare and effectiveness due to a lack of information or poor information remain, particularly among those in restricted settings.

FOUR

Abortion discourses: religion, culture, nation

While the law and health policy on abortion in particular jurisdictions has a direct influence on how and if women access abortion, wider cultural factors influence how these laws and policies are made and interpreted. Debates on abortion are multi-layered and complex, comprising a consideration of institutional factors related to government structure, politics and party systems configuration, as well as the influence of non-government actors such as the medical community, the pro-choice and anti-abortion movements (Engeli, 2012). Schwartz and Tatalovich (2009: 78) argue that cultural factors must also be considered alongside institutional factors. Institutions do not operate in a vacuum but 'through values and norms that make them part of the cultural fabric of a society', with variation in cultural and institutional factors present in different jurisdictions.

Abortion debates often focus on arguments based on supposed religious and cultural values and assumptions, rather than on women's rights or healthcare needs. Religious and cultural norms have huge potential to influence both individual and societal perceptions of abortion and its legality. The terms 'religion' and 'culture' have many points of overlap, are often used interchangeably and may be tied to conceptions of nationality and nation-building. Both religious and cultural narratives can be appealed to in order to oppose abortion and claim that it is not part of a particular society's cultural order. Kozlowska et al (2016), for example, argue that where religion is tied into national identity, it is more likely that restrictive abortion policies will be in place.

This chapter addresses the influence of religion and culture on abortion discourses in societies which have undergone substantial transitions and therefore have attempted to build new and inclusive national identities. Transitions offer unique opportunities to examine changes in conceptions of rights and citizenship, and are typically particularly gendered. Transitions have often been shown to be negative for women, with leaders often promoting traditional or conservative gender norms as a means of building a cohesive national identity (Meintjes et al, 2001).

The examples of Northern Ireland and South Africa – the former having undergone a transition from violent conflict to relative peace, and the latter a transition from apartheid and violent conflict to democracy – exhibit very different outcomes in terms of abortion legislation. However, in both jurisdictions abortion is difficult to access. Discourses on abortion in the two case studies illustrate how women's rights, and in particular, abortion rights, are tied to notions of religion, culture and nation, and as such continue to embed conservative ideas about womanhood in new national identities.

Religious, cultural and national discourses

Religious and cultural norms are often utilised as a device to limit or deny women bodily autonomy (even though we can recognise that gender is not a universal or homogenous concept and that women do not conceive of their rights in the same way globally). Such cultural relativism appeals to conservative interpretations and notions of culture, religion and national identity. Women's rights are particularly subservient to cultural relativism and are viewed as having less universal and global resonance than less gendered rights (Coomaraswamy, 1994). Conservative discourses often suggest that particular societies or communities do not want or welcome abortion, or that it is against a particular religious belief. Stated often and over a period of time this becomes accepted knowledge or fact.

Conservative notions of nations and nationalism have been implicated in developing particular identities for women. Nira Yuval-Davis' (1994) seminal text *Gender and Nation* illustrated women's role as biological reproducers of the nation, rather than being active participants in nation-building, with women being cultural symbols signifying the purity of the nation through their moral virtue. It is assumed that women will both represent the essence of their culture, and reproduce and transmit this to their children. Accordingly, women's behaviour and bodies are regulated and policed to uphold traditional ideals. Abortion, with its assumed rejection of motherhood, overthrows national ideals, and as such can be argued to be in complete contradiction to, or a rejection of, national identity and national ideology. Feminist conceptualisations of citizenship illustrate its gendered nature, with marriage, parenthood and military service forming the basis of what defines modern citizenship in liberal democratic regimes (Pateman, 1988). This sexual citizenship defines women's role as primarily a supportive one in the private domain, and reifies women's identities in relation to the public/private divide and its correspondence in the sexual division of labour (Evans, 2013). Consequently, the state may grant differential freedoms, rights and supports to individuals or groups based on its consideration of sexual citizenship.

In societies which have undergone violent conflict or transition, the call to a conservative national identity can be seen even more clearly, with national identity and traditional gender norms viewed as stabilising factors, and the biological and cultural reproduction of the nation a core concern (Meintjes et al, 2001). Gender identities become entrenched and essentialised, and cultural communities homogenised, leaving little room for diversity in discourse of national and cultural identity. These identities are often created in relation to the 'other' in society, whether that is another ethnic group or a coloniser. Women bear the brunt of such nation-building, particularly with regard to their sexual and reproductive rights, and attempts to transgress these boundaries can be heavily penalised. The implementation of pronatalist policies to reproduce the nation in divided and conflicted societies, is obviously in contradiction to abortion rights. Armed movements from Serbia to Rwanda, Burundi, Japan, Palestine, Turkey and South Sudan have called for women to produce babies 'for the nation' (Palmer and Storeng, 2016).

As noted in the introduction to this chapter, when nationhood is intertwined with religion, the effects become even more pronounced. The relationship between religion and nationalism is complex. Brubaker (2012) suggests four means of understanding the relationship: nationalism as a form of religion, religion as the origin and power of nationalism, religion as part of nationalism and religious forms of nationalism. In Western countries religious morality typically stems from Catholic theology and evangelical Protestantism. Critics point out, however, that historically the anti-abortion policy of the Christian churches has not been consistent (Petchesky, 1986; Rose, 2007). In the sixteenth century, for instance, Pope Gregory XIV did not regard abortion as a mortal sin until the point of quickening, at which the woman felt the foetus moving (ensoulment). This mirrors the legislative position in Ireland during the same time period, during which abortion was considered a minor offence. It was not until the British Offences Against the Person Act 1861 that the distinction between 'un-ensouled' and 'ensouled' foetuses was removed (Kennedy and Gilmartin, 2018).

Levels of religiosity in society have been implicated in the continuance of restrictive abortion laws. Minkenberg (2002) posits that at the individual country level the impact of religion on abortion law and policy can be measured by an analysis of cultural heritage (Catholicism versus Protestantism) and levels of religiosity in a society (church attendance). In Minkenberg's comparative analysis of countries with restrictive and liberal abortion policies, those with high religiosity were more likely to have restrictive laws, while those with low religiosity had liberal laws (Minkenberg, 2002). It was argued that countries exhibiting high Catholic religiosity (for example, Portugal and the Republic of Ireland) had restrictive laws compared to countries with high Protestant religiosity (for example, Sweden and Denmark). While Minkenberg's analysis is useful, others argue that the situation is more complex and dependent on the penetration of moral and religious issues into the political sphere (Durham, 2005; Engeli et al, 2013).

In the twentieth century, as a reaction to increasing legislative change on abortion globally, the Catholic Church attempted to influence relevant international treaties, with the goal of halting any movement to legitimise abortion. It sought alliances with unlikely partners such as Libya and Iran, countries which also aimed to reduce access to abortion. In 1994, at the International Conference on Population and Development (ICPD) in Cairo, the Catholic Church, under the leadership of the Holy See, lobbied against policies related to contraceptive use and abortion, resulting in a more conservative content of the Cairo Declaration than had been anticipated (Chong and Troy, 2011). It used similar tactics in later years in parallel with the US administration, which sought to maintain the support of the Christian right for the Republican President George W. Bush in lobbying for the phrase 'reproductive health' to be excluded from the Millennium Development Goals (MDGs) in 2001.

Later United Nations' declarations sought to reverse these moves, and in 2005 access to reproductive health was added to the maternal health section of the MDGs (Guns, 2013). However, delayed focus on reproductive health over a five-year period led to a reduction in resources for associated programmes and contributed to slow progress on the MDG targets. Hulme (2009a, 2009b) argues that this 'unholy' alliance led to the marginalisation of maternal health, and contributed negatively to efforts to reduce extreme income poverty and gender inequality, decrease child and maternal mortality rates, and tackle HIV/AIDS incidence rates.

In Latin America, conservative Catholic theorists repackaged religious ideologies in secular rights-based discourse, with campaigns against public sex education and sexual health services resulting in 'an orchestrated backlash against Latin American reproductive and sexual rights movements' (Morgan, 2014: 2). Evidence indicates that the behaviour of the largely Catholic population in Latin America conflicts with the teachings of the Church: divorce, contraceptive use and abortion are all prevalent. In addition, critics have argued that the Catholic Church has sought to challenge some moral infractions with less zeal than others (for instance, child sexual abuse) (Bloomer and O'Dowd, 2014; Morgan, 2014).

Among other faiths, nuanced views on abortion are evident. For instance, although Orthodox Jews are opposed to most abortions, those aligned with conservative and reformist traditions of Judaism tend to be largely supportive of safe and legal abortion. Despite Protestantism's evangelical movement currently holding a restrictive stance on abortion, this has not always been so. Dudley (2011) has demonstrated, for instance, that among evangelical churches in the US, liberal views on abortion were common up until the 1960s. Documenting debates on abortion within leading Christian publications such as *Christianity Today*, Dudley (2011) notes that leading theologians argued that the foetus had no soul. This later moved to a position of abortion as 'wrong', though permissible in cases of rape and incest. This stance changed in the late 1960s and 1970s, when conservative religious voters sought to exert a stronger influence on politics (Petroni, 2011). While this change was led at first by the Catholic Church, Protestant churches soon became involved, resulting in several anti-abortion organisations forming during the 1970s and 1980s. The Republican Party's liberal policy on abortion of the 1970s was soon replaced by anti-abortion rhetoric (Rose, 2007).

The development of this positioning on abortion furthers the argument that the political impact of religious belief is highly dependent on social context (Durham, 2005). It also serves to focus attention on the perspective that a liberal position on abortion is not in contradiction to religious belief. The rhetoric of political debate often assumes commonality between religiosity and anti-abortion views, yet evidence suggests otherwise, as noted above in relation to South America. It is argued that the same is true of abortion for many Catholics around the world (McMurtie et al, 2012; Williams, 2013; Clements, 2014). Indeed, there are many conservative faith-based organisations who view abortion as immoral, but there are others from a liberal position, such as Catholics for Choice, the Religious Institute, the Religious Coalition for Reproductive Choice and the Latin American Council of Churches, who argue that it is immoral to restrict access to abortion.

In relation to an Islamic perspective on abortion, Hessini (2016) rightly points out that while restrictive laws on abortion exist in Muslim-majority contexts, many of these emanate from colonial times, and not from Shari'a or Islamic law. As with other faiths, viewing those from a Muslim faith and Muslim-majority contexts as a monolithic block is unwise. Hessini highlights the example of Tunisia, which reformed its law on abortion before France and the US, and where abortion is largely accepted in society (Hessini, 2016: 72). Female scholars, such as Fatima Mernissi, have played a significant role in challenging patriarchal norms ascribed to religious texts by, for instance, undertaking archival work and uncovering feminist role models in Muslim history (Hessini, 2016: 73).

Activist organisations in Indonesia, Morocco, Egypt and Malaysia have led the way in engaging with local communities in promoting equality and reproductive health education, by undertaking programmes which interpret religious texts from a feminist perspective, educating women about human rights and how these rights can be informed by Islamic traditions (Hessini, 2016). Such evidence assists in examining the positioning of women in modern society and the norms that have led to their marginalisation within many societies.

Abortion stigma

Evident within the consideration of discourse about abortion is abortion stigma, which is defined by Kumar et al (2009: 628) as 'a negative attribute ascribed to women who seek to terminate a pregnancy that marks them, internally or externally, as inferior to the ideal of "womanhood"'. The concept of abortion stigma largely emerged within the literature in the early part of the twenty-first century, with much remaining unknown about specific processes that create and propagate it, and how it appears within different contexts. Commentators have argued that inherent within a consideration of abortion stigma are societal norms of gender (Cockrill and Nack, 2013). In societies where motherhood is synonymous with womanhood, abortion becomes viewed as an abhorrent transgression: to have an abortion is to reject motherhood and procreation. This positioning of abortion ignores the fact that many who have abortions are already mothers or intend to be in the future, and thus are only rejecting it at that point, for that particular pregnancy.

Studies suggest that in settings where abortion stigma is prevalent women experience negative consequences of both felt (internalised) stigma and enacted (experienced) stigma from others. This may lead to abortion concealment, with disclosure being problematic among friends and family members. This in turn contributes to isolation and negative judgments of self-worth. It may impact negatively on women's help-seeking behaviour and also contributes to societal silence about abortion (Cockrill and Nack, 2013). Abortion stigma has been identified in societies where abortion is restricted but also in societies where it is more freely available. It is affected by community values, societal and health professional norms around acceptability of who should have access to abortion, whether those with multiple abortions are viewed as acceptable and so on. Lesley Hoggart's body of work with young women in England and Wales illustrates how community and family values on abortion and motherhood influence both felt and enacted stigma (Hoggart, 2012, 2017; Hoggart et al, 2015, 2016). These studies also illustrate that stigma can be resisted by women, and that this typically occurs in situations where the decision to have an abortion is regarded as morally sound.

Abortion stigma is not just experienced by those seeking abortion, but also by abortion providers. This is typically manifested in public displays of hostility outside abortion clinics and in their own communities, but also, in some instances, from within their profession and health setting (Harris et al, 2013; Debbink et al, 2016; Teffo and Rispel, 2017). The impact on professionals can vary from a reluctance to pursue abortion provision in the longer term to psychosocial issues. Alternatively, abortion providers may resist stigma too, and instead seek to advocate for de-stigmatisation. Dr Willie Parker is a prime example of this, following in the footsteps of peers such as Dr George Tiller, who was murdered by an anti-abortion extremist while attending church. Dr Parker firmly advocates that he is doing 'God's work' by providing abortions. He rejects the stigmatisation of abortion and argues that conservative forces aiming to restrict abortion are doing so based on deeply flawed discourses (Parker, 2017).

Conservative global discourses which aim to restrict women's access to safe and legal abortion are replicated within the two case study contexts. Both use narratives of specific cultural ideologies. In Northern Ireland this is linked to ethnoreligious forms of national identity and unification of a divided society, whereas in South Africa discourses on community cohesiveness and postcolonialism are utilised to justify opposition to abortion. The outcome of these framings of abortion is to stifle legislative reform in Northern Ireland and to contribute to stigma and access to safe abortion in the South African context.

Case Study: Northern Ireland

Northern Ireland is located in the northwest of Europe and forms the north region of the island of Ireland as a separate jurisdiction which is part of the United Kingdom (UK). It has a population of approximately 1.8 million, with the population being almost equally split between Catholicism and Protestantism. As part of the UK, the health system operates within the National Health Service (NHS), a free at the point of delivery service, funded by government via a taxation system. Northern Ireland has the smallest economy of the four countries of the UK (England, Scotland and Wales constituting the other three); however, throughout the 1990s, the Northern Irish economy grew faster than in the rest of the UK, due in part to the rapid Celtic Tiger growth within the Republic of Ireland and as a result of the peace process which followed a period of intense conflict lasting over three decades. Economic growth did not benefit all of society, however, with significant socioeconomic deprivation and the legacy of the conflict both evident in the early part of the twenty-first century.

Northern Ireland is commonly described as a divided society. With a distinct ethnoreligious national identity based on a hybrid combination of conservative Catholic and evangelical Protestant religiosity, the region underwent 30 years of violent civil conflict between 1969 and 1998, based on its constitutional status as part of the UK. While an overall downward trend in church attendance has been observed in the last three decades, religious affiliation remains evident (Hayes and Dowds, 2010) and is notably higher than elsewhere in the UK. A survey carried out in 2016 identified that in terms of religious affiliation, 19% of respondents stated they had no religion (ARK, 2017); this is in stark contrast to 50% of respondents to the British Social Attitudes survey carried out during the same time period (Lee, 2017). The religiosity in society exerts an influence even on those who are not actively religious; religious ideas, beliefs, traditions and symbols continue to give meaning and structure to social life, and the penetration of religion into everyday life often goes unnoticed (Mitchell, 2006).

Northern Ireland's governance operates on consociational principles, including a cross-community, power-sharing executive with minority veto rights and cultural respect for both Protestant and Catholic communities. Ethnonational identity is specifically linked to religious affiliation. In effect, party political structures have developed on ethnoreligious grounds and voters are positioned as solely focused on protecting ethnic interests (Taylor, 2009). The right to veto and the parity of consent model positions all issues along the ethnonational divide and makes passing legislation more difficult. In the consociational context, both the formal representation of women in politics and gender issues being on the political agenda are difficult to ensure based on the primacy of ethnonationalism (Kennedy et al, 2016). This has been described as the 'lowest common denominator' approach to law and policymaking (Gray and Birrell, 2012).

Since the Good Friday Agreement of 1998, which was the culmination of a lengthy peace process, four main parties have dominated the political landscape Northern Ireland. The Democratic Unionist Party (DUP) and the Ulster Unionist Party (UUP) are the core Protestant/Unionist parties, and Sinn Féin (SF) and the Social Democratic and Labour Party (SDLP) are the principal Catholic/Nationalist parties. Non-sectarian parties organise in Northern Ireland but are stymied by the sectarian nature of voting patterns. There is evidence to suggest that religious convictions (and the perceived religious convictions of party supporters) influence the development of party policies and the decision-making of some politicians (Tonge et al, 2014).

Mitchell (2006) positions the role of the Catholic and Protestant churches in the formal political arena as a mutually beneficial relationship. The roles of the Catholic Church and Protestant Churches are distinct in their direct influence in politics. The Catholic Church is closely located within community social lives and has a particular role in education, whereas there is more overt overlap between Protestant Churches and political actors (Mitchell, 2006). Politicians, aware of church influence, work in partnership with churches, and provide them with a platform to promote their perspectives on social and moral issues. Politicians rarely oppose church perspectives or teachings; a notable recent exception has been the open support from some politicians for same-sex marriage (Black, 2015). Sinn Féin has a tumultuous relationship with the Catholic Church. The party's stance on abortion has largely been regarded as vague until 2018. At its 2017 Ard Fheis (annual party conference), its position was clarified to include support for the availability of abortion in cases where a woman's life, or physical or mental health is at serious risk, in addition to cases of fatal foetal abnormalities and cases of sexual crime. In June 2018, following the success of the referendum to repeal the 8th Amendment in the Republic of Ireland just weeks previously (as discussed in Chapter Two), the party adopted a new policy which set out to match the proposed legislation in the Republic of Ireland, allowing for abortion up to 12 weeks, with restricted access thereafter. In the lead up to the June 2018 Ard Fheis, party leaders made clear that as an all-Ireland party, it would seek reform in Northern Ireland and that political parties who had yet to adopt a liberal approach, such as the DUP, were failing society. In adopting this position, Sinn Fein were effectively also signalling its distance from the Catholic Church.

Research focusing on evangelical Protestant groups within Northern Ireland, such as the Caleb Foundation (a religious think tank formed in 1998), illustrates their relationship to the political arena. Ganiel (2006) relates that evangelical groups have reframed their political projects, moving away from constitutional concerns towards moral and social issues. This is typified by an organisation which has emerged in recent years, the Evangelical Alliance, which has received significant media attention for its campaigns on a broad range of moral and social issues. Abortion and same-sex marriage continue to be social issues which differ legally from the wider UK context, and the continuance of this disparity is lobbied for by such groups. Catholic and Protestant church leaders have lobbied against abortion on a regular basis, occasionally in joint efforts. In 2008, when there was an opportunity in Westminster to extend the Abortion Act 1967 to Northern Ireland, leaders of the main churches wrote to all UK MPs asking them to oppose the amendment in order to respect the wishes of the people of Northern Ireland and allow locally elected politicians in the Northern Ireland Assembly to legislate (Bloomer and O'Dowd, 2014).

Although religion is utilised as a divisive tool in Northern Ireland, defining political boundaries and indicating the 'other', attitudes towards any relaxation of the law surrounding abortion can be viewed as a means of unifying religious and political factions in the region. A unanimous rejection of abortion by both Catholics and Protestants is often noted throughout political debate on the subject within the devolved assembly. In fact, in the midst of negotiations on the Good Friday Agreement, an all-party delegation met with the then Prime Minister, John Major, to lobby against any extension of the 1967 act to Northern Ireland (Thomson, 2018), and one of the first devolved assembly debates confirmed that the assembly would not be extending the act. Attitudes towards abortion were concurrently framed along cross-party, cross-community and cross-religious bases. This was despite evidence in public opinion polls which indicated otherwise, as discussed below.

In the UK, abortion continues to be treated as a criminal act under the Offences Against the Person Act 1861. Abortion law was reformed in England, Scotland and Wales in 1967, to permit abortion under certain circumstances. Subsequent attempts from Westminster to introduce the law in Northern Ireland have been unsuccessful. Most notable were the efforts of Emily Thornberry and then Diane Abbott, both Labour MPs, who sought to add an amendment to the Human Fertilisation and Embryology Bill 2008 to extend the Abortion Act 1967 to Northern Ireland. The then Minister for Health, Alan Johnson, opposed this, stating that to do so would have a destabilising effect on the Northern Ireland peace process (Bloomer, 2013). More recently other Labour MPs such as Stella Creasy have sought to highlight the disparity women in Northern Ireland face in accessing abortion compared to those living elsewhere in the UK.

The absence of reform in Northern Ireland has allowed for case law to set the circumstances under which abortion may take place. This specifies that abortion is permitted where the woman's life is in danger or the pregnancy poses a 'real and serious, permanent or long term' risk to her health (Bloomer and Fegan, 2014). This restrictive law results in an average of 45 legal abortions per year being carried out in Northern Ireland, which forces an average of 1,000 women per year to travel to England (until mid-2017 those who travelled had to pay as private patients despite being UK tax payers) (Bloomer et al, 2017a). Others, still, purchase the abortion pill from organisations such as Women on Web and Women Help Women and self-abort at home, or accessed abortions from Marie Stopes International's Belfast clinic (which provided early medical abortion during 2012–17). In recent years, prosecutions have occurred of those who have self-aborted at home and activists' workplaces have been targeted in the search for abortion pills. Flawed draft guidelines issued by the Department of Health in 2013 resulted in a climate of fear among health professionals, and while revised guidelines have been issued, the chill factor from the previous version remains (Bloomer et al, 2016). This, combined with prosecutions, means that those seeking abortion are faced with multiple barriers and abortion stigma is prevalent. As discussed in the next chapter, an inquiry conducted by the UN Committee on the Elimination of Discrimination Against Women, published in 2018, determined that women and girls in Northern Ireland had experienced grave and systemic violation of their rights as a result of restricted access to abortion (Bloomer et al, 2018b; CEDAW, 2018).

Political discourse on abortion in Northern Ireland

Between its inception in 1998 and 2014 the Northern Ireland Assembly held four major debates on abortion. These sessions centred on the issue of legal reform or policy issues such as guidelines for medical staff. Each debate has been dominated by a prevailing moral conservatism, with a largely anti-abortion rhetoric. One of the most notable aspects of these debates has been the continual framing of the issue as one which cuts across ethnonational and ethnoreligious lines (Bloomer and Pierson, 2016). For example, during a debate in 2013 the term 'cross-community' was used 10 times by Jonathan Bell of the DUP in reference to opposition to abortion.

The debate in 2013 centred on the opening of a Marie Stopes International (MSI) clinic in Belfast in October 2012, with a proposed amendment to the Justice Bill in March 2013 seeking to stop private organisations from offering abortion services. Although the discussion might have been expected to focus on the use of private providers for public health services, there was a predominance of reference to religion throughout the debate. References to the similarity of positions taken by both Protestant and Catholic Churches throughout the island of Ireland was noted and the phrase 'across the religious spectrum/community' used repeatedly. More overt religious references were also observed, including the DUP referring to the Minister for Justice (David Ford, Alliance Party) as 'Pontius Pilate', while Chris Lyttle from the Alliance Party criticised the debate as an 'abuse of religion for political purposes ... [which] would not have been out of place in a court of Pharisees' (Hansard, 2013: 73).

Direct reference to religious belief and political decision-making is evident. Politicians such as Pat Ramsey of the SDLP, noted below, indicate that faith must be the core factor in any decision regarding abortion, therefore negating any possibility of taking account of evidence or changing public opinion:

> My culture, background and faith mean that I — not just politically, but personally — want to be a champion for the unborn child. I want to protect the unborn child. I want to ensure that I prevent abortions. (Hansard, 2013: 54)

Faith also becomes a bargaining tool for arguing against an evidence base in policy and legislation. The language of political debate mirrors that of draft healthcare policy guidelines on abortion, with constant reference to the 'unborn' and 'mothers' rather than the 'foetus' and 'women'.

The resulting political discourse is one which positions abortion as abhorrent and immoral to everyone in Northern Ireland and makes the assumption that the whole population ascribe to similar interpretations of religious beliefs. The quote below is illustrative of such debate:

> Across the island of Ireland, we share a common bond in seeking to protect and provide the best care for mothers and unborn children. We are recognised globally as one of the premier providers of maternal care. That this common political bond has been replicated across our religious communities is demonstrated by support from the Church of Ireland, the Presbyterian Church in Ireland and the Catholic Church. People ask what a shared future looks like, and I point to this moment of an SDLP, DUP and Ulster Unionist bringing forward proposed legislation related to the most basic of human rights: the right to life. (Paul Givan, DUP, quoted in Hansard, 2013: 9)

This quote exemplifies the ease with which politicians conflate religious belief with political affiliation and national identity. Givan emphasises that the views of the main churches are in line with the views of three of the larger political parties and therefore with the people of Northern Ireland. As a result, the continual framing of opposition to abortion as an issue which unites the whole of Northern Ireland (and the island of Ireland) assumes a consistency of religious belief and silences those who may hold more nuanced or liberal views towards abortion. The high degree of religious observance and cultural affiliation to religion in Northern Ireland, coupled with the presentation of abortion as an issue which is against religious beliefs, ensured that alternative perspectives on abortion were marginalised within the political domain. As a result, positions became increasingly polarised, with any opinion which was not consistently against abortion being labelled as immoral by politicians hostile to reform.

However, public opinion polls paint a more nuanced position on abortion than the black and white nature of political debate. Repeated polls since the mid-1990s demonstrate a certain level of support for legal reform (FPA et al, 2010). The Northern Ireland Life and Times Survey indicated broad support for reform (Gray, 2017), and a study of trade union members in 2017 exhibited similar support for reform and decriminalisation (Bloomer et al, 2017b).

In the Northern Ireland context, conservative religious discourse and evidence-based policy are inconsistent with each other, with conservative discourse trumping evidence in legislation and policymaking. Consequently, the language of political debate highlights that politicians are not representing the health needs of their constituents but instead representing a hegemonic and conservative ethnoreligious faith view which they extrapolate to be the belief of the whole of Northern Ireland. As such, opposition to abortion has been typically presented as a unifying identity in the divided society and part of inclusive nation-building. Recent debates have evidenced more nuance and divergence on the issue; Sinn Fein's policy change in 2018 indicated their support for reform, however the main unionist party (the DUP) remains resistant to legal reform and has yet to acknowledge subtle complexities in the debate on abortion access.

Case study: South Africa

South Africa is the southernmost country in the continent of Africa and has a population of approximately 56 million people. South Africa is a multi-ethnic society encompassing a wide variety of cultures, languages and religions. About 80% of South Africans are of sub-Saharan African ancestry, divided among a variety of ethnic groups speaking different African languages, nine of which have official status. The remaining population consists of Africa's largest communities of European (white), Asian (Indian) and multiracial ancestry. South Africa is a largely Christian country, with a small percentage of the population practising Islam, Hinduism, Judaism and other religions; 15% of people indicate that they are non-religious.

South Africa underwent one of the most well-known transitions to democracy globally when apartheid, and the violent conflict which accompanied it, ended in the early 1990s. The system of apartheid, which classed people into three races, was a furtherance of racial segregation introduced in the Dutch and British colonial periods. South Africa is considered a success in terms of the inclusion of women and gender issues within the constitution, and the descriptive and substantive representation of women in formal politics (Seidman, 1999; Waylen, 2010). This success is largely attributed to visible and powerful feminist organising and strategising, and links between antiracist and feminist movements. However, rates of rape, sexual violence and coercive sex are high, as are rates of family and intimate partner violence (Commission for Gender Equality, 2014).

Despite comprehensive equality provisions written into the South African constitution, issues of inequality permeate society. Life expectancy is 55 years for males and 66 for females (WHO, 2017b). It is a middle- to low-income country, with wide disparity in income equalities. In recent decades, the South African government has invested significant resources in its health systems, such as those dedicated to HIV/AIDs and Tuberculosis and immunisation programmes. However, health inequalities are evident, with the wealthy making use of a well-developed private healthcare system that employs 55% of doctors and most specialists. Investment in health has resulted in a decrease in under-five and neonatal mortality (42 and 14 per 1,000 live births respectively in 2013/14) but these rates are still high in comparison with other countries of similar socioeconomic status. Maternal mortality ratios also remain high, estimated at 269 deaths per 100,000 live births (WHO, 2017b). Other deaths are attributable to non-communicable causes, with risks from alcohol abuse and obesity prevalent. Despite access to clean water being common, environmental challenges which impact on health, such as those associated with the reliance on coal, are evident (WHO, 2017b).

Access to abortion in South Africa

In terms of access to abortion, South Africa presents as a state with liberal laws but persistently high levels of unsafe abortion and concerning levels of maternal mortality. During the apartheid period, unsafe abortions and maternal death were common, and treating such cases had a significant impact on scarce health resources. In the 1960s this led to calls from medical professionals for law reform to take place to enable safe legal abortions to be provided. Such calls went unheeded. Instead, the state sought to prosecute those who were providing illegal abortions; this included targeting one of the country's leading gynaecologists, Derk Crichton (Hodes, 2016). Such high-profile cases were viewed as a warning to Crichton and his colleagues' main client group: young white women. During Crichton's trial, the media exposed details of the private lives of these women in lurid tones, subjecting them to intense public scrutiny and thus punishing them for flagrant breaking of social and sexual norms (Hodes, 2016). Prosecutions of providers continued throughout the 1970s. The clampdown affected lower- and middle-class women, who unlike their affluent peers were unable to travel abroad to access abortions in the Netherlands and the UK. Instead, these women accessed abortions at backstreet clinics (Hodes, 2016). Added to this debate were attempts to curb the size of the black population. While this contributed to debate about overpopulation, the state's main focus appears to have been on preventing abortions among the white population; they were less concerned with the high levels of unsafe abortion among the black population (Hodes, 2016). A law introduced in 1975 sought to place additional regulations on providers; however, clandestine abortions remained common, with doctors commonly providing them in public hospitals (Hodes, 2016), and others continuing the use of herbal concoctions and other means of inducing abortion.

Resistance to the restricted access to abortion was challenged by women's organisations, but such organisations largely remained on the periphery until the transition phase from the apartheid regime to democracy. Typically, the efforts of these organisations had been labelled as efforts of liberal feminism, imported from Western societies and dominated by white middle-class women, and a distraction from the fight for democracy. Activists sought to reposition access to abortion as part of political emancipation, and argued that the apartheid regime had sought to silence and isolate the issue of abortion access. As a result of activists' efforts, support for legal abortion became a key policy of the African National Congress (ANC), the dominant political party in the new regime (Hodes, 2016: 84). Recognition of the impact of unsafe abortion formed a core element of the need for legal reform. In the ensuing public debate this also led to a key argument that access to safe abortion was predominantly a health issue.

The new law, the Choice on Termination of Pregnancy Act, was passed in 1996 and came into effect in early 1997. The law is regarded as adopting a liberal approach to abortion: abortion on request is allowed up to 12 weeks of gestation; no parental consent is required; both midwives and medics are permitted to carry out abortions, though abortion after 13 weeks can only be carried out by medics (an amendment in 2004 allowed for nurses to carry out abortions up until 12 weeks' gestation). After 13 weeks, provision of abortion is subject to a list of conditions such as:

> that continuing with the pregnancy … poses a risk to a women's mental or physical health; that the foetus is malformed; that the pregnancy resulted from rape or incest; or that the pregnancy would have a harmful effect on the woman's social and economic status. Abortion can be performed after 20 weeks of gestation if a woman's life is in danger or if the foetus is malformed. (Government of South Africa, 1996)

The inclusion of the woman's social and economic status was regarded as particularly important: it was not defined within the law and thus allowed medics leeway in offering abortion. This, coupled with abortions being permitted up to 12 weeks on request, placed the law among the most liberal in the world.

Deaths from unsafe abortion decreased by between 51.3 and 94.8% during the period 1994–2001. The broad range is due to uncertainty over 1994 data; however, the authors suggest that a 91% reduction is likely (Jewkes and Rees, 2008: 250). The majority of abortions (70%) are now performed by midwives and nurses in the first trimester. Providers include public hospitals, private clinics and other nongovernmental facilities. While initially departmental Ministers for Health were clearly pro-choice, in more recent years the leadership has been less clear-cut, and abortion policy has become less of a priority. This is exemplified by a change in how abortion-related deaths are reported, with data merged with HIV-related deaths and not disaggregated (Trueman and Magwentshu, 2013). Worth noting, too, is that there have been several attempts to restrict the Choice on Termination of Pregnancy Act, though none have been successful.

Despite the decrease in death rates following the introduction of the law, unsafe abortion persists in South Africa. Research estimates that over half of abortions are still unsafe (Sedgh et al, 2011). Those most at risk include women in lower socioeconomic groups, those living with HIV, those who are black and those living in the provinces of Gauteng, Limpopo or KwaZulu-Natal. In contrast, higher socioeconomic groups, those living without HIV, those who are white, and/ or those residing in other provinces are least at risk (Mosley et al, 2017: 918).

Multiple barriers to safe abortion have been identified; for instance, a lack of local provision or fears over anonymity may force women to travel considerable distances to access an abortion (Trueman and Magwentshu, 2013). A study of abortion provision in five public sector hospitals in the Western Cape province determined that women encountered a number of problematic issues when accessing abortion (Grossman et al, 2011). Typically, this included delays of two to four weeks from requesting an abortion to it being carried out, pushing women into second trimester abortions which thus resulted in the need for more invasive procedures and longer stays in hospital. The study also found that few women received analgesia, and as a result over 50% experienced extreme/ high levels of pain. Such challenges were ascribed to a lack of qualified staff and resources. The authors also suggest that punitive attitudes towards abortion from providers may be at play (Grossman et al, 2011: 9). Conscientious objection was identified by Trueman and Magwentshu (2013) as a key factor in restricted access to abortion, and the absence of clear guidance from provincial health departments was viewed as contributing to this. In addition, there remains among some communities a lack of knowledge about access to free abortions, and a fear of discrimination or confidentiality breach by health workers (Trueman and Magwentshu, 2013; Mosley et al, 2017). It should be recognised too that inadequate resources, inadequate training and long waiting lists place a particular burden on abortion providers.

In terms of wider society, research indicates that there are broadly positive attitudes towards availability of abortion but that differences emerge when considering the argument of moral acceptability and bodily autonomy (Mosley et al, 2017). This is exemplified in accepting views of abortion on the grounds of sexual crime, foetal anomaly, danger to health, if living with HIV or if it is the first abortion. In contrast, those seeking abortion who are unmarried or adolescent, on low incomes, or requesting a non-first abortion are regarded in a negative manner (Mosley et al, 2017).

Scholars have sought to unpack how abortion is constructed in South Africa, with a particular focus on why hostility to it remains. Their findings indicate that variation occurs, and is dependent on a range of factors. One study conducted in a rural area identified that even when participants articulated benefits to improved access to abortion, abortion was, in relation to their cultural values, constructed in a hostile manner, as an act of killing and associated with colonialist interventions. Thus opposition to abortion was seen as defending the community's culture (Macleod et al, 2011). Improved access to abortion was constructed as symbolic of a range of changes that had a negative impact on the community's traditions and cultural values. It was also evident that issues of loss of gendered and generational power relations were at play in how abortion was constructed. Abortion was seen as representing a rejection of the natural state of motherhood, as a symbol of promiscuity and as a challenge to the reified status of marriage. It also represented a disconnect between older and younger generations. In urban areas, among a different profile of research participants, university students, a more liberal approach to abortion was observed. Those that were hostile to abortion identified that this stemmed from a particular moralistic standpoint, again referring to abortion as murder; typically, this was ascribed to religious teachings, with many students noting the influence of the type of school they had attended, for example, Catholic (Gresh and Maharaj, 2014).

Conclusions

The two case studies presented above illustrate factors influencing access to safe abortion other than legal positions. Religious, national and cultural discourses are utilised as a means either to stifle legal change or to continue stigmatisation, which often leads to unsafe abortion practices and, in fact, higher rates of abortion in the country in question. Such discourses stem from a belief that abortion does not happen if it is illegal, and that it is completely contrary to particular beliefs and cultural regimes.

The utilisation of such discourses in societies emerging from transition is complex. Often nation-building is presented as a means to unify communities and to distance the nation from the 'other', whether that be a colonising force or another ethnic group. While national discourses can be liberatory, often for women and gender orders they are not. Such nation-building, however, conceptualises a form of citizenship which continues to be both gendered and exclusionary, affording lesser rights to women than men. Often such debates are impacted by race, and as discussed in Chapter Seven, result in multiple reproductive oppressions.

With a need to provide equality for those who have been made unequal in a particular society, challenging conservative narratives of womanhood and women's bodily autonomy is difficult. It can be labelled as an affront to the national and religious identity of the group, and a form of cultural imperialism. This must be challenged, however. The most useful and powerful means to do this should be based on factual and experiential evidence from women in a particular society of their reproductive lives and needs. Such a challenge begins to break down cultural hegemonies and beliefs about women's role in society.

FIVE

International interventions

While law and policy on abortion is formed at the national level and access should be provided by the state, there are situations where international intervention into national abortion law and abortion care is necessary. This chapter explores two types of such interventions: human rights-based interventions, whereby international and regional bodies monitor state compliance with particular human rights treaties to provide recommendations or formally binding decisions, and humanitarian interventions, whereby in situations of crisis and conflict the international community intervenes to ensure that women have access to reproductive health services.

International human rights-based interventions in abortion have provided opinion, judgments and clarity on issues such as access to abortion, safety of care and interpretation of law. What the international sphere has refrained from doing, however, is to guarantee a right to abortion for women who choose it, as an aspect of equality and self-determination (Zampas and Gher, 2008). This has focused abortion within a physical health and safety discourse, rather than one of equality and agency. Since the mid-1990s, international and regional human rights instruments, treaty bodies and commissions have established that lack of access to abortion violates human rights norms in a number of circumstances. Most importantly, this body of interpretation provides a legitimate framework for governments, civil society actors and activists to either enact or lobby for abortion law reform within states. Use of human rights interpretations on abortion can be seen in cases and national law reform in countries as diverse as Colombia, Nepal, Rwanda and Spain (Fine et al, 2017).

Conflict and humanitarian crises continue to affect millions of people per year. Women and girls are disproportionality affected by conflict and crisis, suffering the same injustices as men and boys but with added layers often arising because of their sexual and reproductive capacities. The UN reports that there are currently over 128 million people worldwide in need of humanitarian assistance (UNOCHA, 2017). Of those, a quarter are women and girls between the ages of 15 and 49, and one in five of these women and girls is likely to be pregnant. Documentation of the rise in rates of sexual violence during conflict and displacement adds an extra layer of complexity into reproductive health service provision for women and girls in, or escaping conflict.

This chapter considers the development of international and regional human rights norms on abortion and the potential future directions that will define international human rights norms on abortion. It also explores how human rights norms have been used to challenge national abortion laws, with particular focus on the Philippines and the Convention on the Elimination of Discrimination Against Women Optional Protocol Inquiry. The second half of the chapter considers the international humanitarian response to reproductive and sexual health challenges in conflict and crisis situations, focusing on the International Planned Parenthood Federation (IPPF) and its humanitarian crisis unit.

International human rights law

Despite the first international treaty on human rights, the Universal Declaration (UDHR), being drafted in 1948, followed by a number of international and regional instruments including the Convention on the Elimination of Discrimination Against Women (CEDAW) in 1979, reproductive rights, and in particular abortion, did not feature in international debates until the 1990s. However, it is clear that the wording of the UDHR specifically considered life to begin from birth not conception, indicating that the drafting states were aware of the potential difficulties of granting rights to the foetus. The 1994 International Conference on Population and Development's Programme of Action called on governments to tackle unsafe abortion and ensure access to legal abortions and abortion care, and was the first time that states explicitly recognised that 'reproductive rights are human rights' (Zampas, 2016). The Beijing Platform for Action in 1995 followed up on this by calling on governments to review punitive laws on abortion and to ensure that abortion was safe and accessible.

In terms of regional documents, the only legally binding document to explicitly call for women's right to abortion is the Protocol on the Rights of Women in Africa (African Women's Protocol), adopted by the African Union on 11 July 2003. It augments the African Charter on Human and Peoples' Rights 1981 (African Charter). The protocol states that:

> State Parties shall take all appropriate measures to ... protect the reproductive rights of women by authorising medical abortion in cases of sexual assault, rape, incest, and where

the continued pregnancy endangers the mental and physical health of the mother or the life of the mother or the foetus.

In 2008, the Council of Europe made a non-legally binding statement on abortion rights. Issued by the Committee on Equal Opportunities for Women and Men, and entitled 'Access to Safe and Legal Abortion in Europe', it calls upon member states to decriminalise abortion; guarantee women's effective exercise of their right to safe and legal abortion; remove restrictions that hinder access to abortion; and adopt evidence-based sexual and reproductive health strategies and policies, such as access to contraception, and compulsory age-appropriate and gender-sensitive sex and relationship education for young people. This particularly progressive statement on abortion can be viewed as an attempt to harmonise the differing abortion laws which exist throughout Europe. However, the European Court of Human Rights itself (the ECtHR) is reluctant to explicitly confirm a right to abortion, leaving states a large margin of appreciation in making abortion laws but ensuring through a number of cases that women must be able to access services within the laws of the particular state.

Under the UN's treaty monitoring system, committees are established by each of the key international treaties and periodically report on a country's human rights obligations with concluding observations offered. The committees issue 'General Comments' or 'General Recommendations' on an as-needed basis, to elaborate on the treaties' broadly worded human rights guarantees and to help states understand their obligations under various treaty provisions. For example, the Human Rights Committee (HRC), the interpretive body of the International Covenant on Civil and Political Rights (ICCPR), emphasises in General Comment No. 28 on equality of rights between men and women, that when reporting on the right to life protected by Article 6, states should 'give information on any measures taken by the State to help women prevent unwanted pregnancies, and to ensure that they do not have to undergo life-threatening clandestine abortions'. General Comment No. 28 also considers laws or policies where states impose a legal duty upon doctors and other health personnel to report cases of women who have undergone abortion, a potential violation of the right to life (Article 6), and the prohibition of torture and cruel, inhuman or degrading treatment or punishment (Article 7). The HRC has also noted the links between illegal and unsafe abortion and maternal mortality, and the effect of unsafe abortion on women's health and wellbeing.

The CEDAW Committee has also made a number of direct statements to countries on abortion. For example, in its 2006 Concluding Observations to Mexico, concern was expressed that abortion remained one of the leading causes of maternal mortality, despite legalisation of abortion in some contexts, due to lack of access to safe abortion services and inadequate access to a wide range of contraception, including emergency contraception. The committee has made a number of statements on the Republic of Ireland and Northern Ireland, and notably, within the periodic review procedures, recommendations to change the law on the island have become more explicit in recent years. For example, in 1999 the CEDAW Committee noted in its periodic review of the UK, 'with concern that the Abortion Act 1967 does not extend to Northern Ireland where, with limited exceptions, abortion continues to be illegal'. It recommended that 'the Government initiate a process of public consultation in Northern Ireland on reform of the abortion law', then in 2013, it recommended that 'the State party should expedite the amendment of the anti-abortion law in Northern Ireland with a view to decriminalise abortion' (CEDAW, 1999: 8; 2013: 9–10).

Recommendations to remove restrictions on abortion also fall under the headings of privacy, liberty and inhuman treatment. For example, the HRC has argued that states which impose a legal duty upon doctors and health personnel to report cases of women who have undergone abortion fail to guarantee women's right to enjoy privacy on the basis of equality with men, and that such provisions constitute discrimination against women. A similar point on the right to privacy is found in Article 17 of the ICCPR and Article 8 of the European Convention on Human Rights (ECHR). It is noted that restrictions on abortion mean that women are denied the right to make private decisions that affect their bodily autonomy and are refused the right to self-determination. The ICCPR has focused on the right to liberty and security of the person – Article 5 of the ECHR and Article 9 of the ICCPR can also be applied to cases of forcing a woman, by threat of criminal sanction, to carry a foetus to full term. This is a profound interference with a woman's body and thus an infringement on security of the person.

There have been four individual complaints to date brought before UN treaty bodies claiming violations from restrictive abortion laws; these have concerned cases of foetal anomaly and sexual crimes. Three cases were presented before the Human Rights Committee (ICCPR) and one at the CEDAW Committee. All cases were ruled in favour of the complainants. This included the KL v. Peru case, whereby the

ICCPR held that the denial of a therapeutic abortion caused 'mental suffering' and amounted to a violation of the prohibition on torture or cruel, inhuman or degrading treatment. The committee did not address the restrictive law; however, the case is important, as its wide definition of health includes mental as well as physical health. In the case of Mellet v Ireland in 2016 (a case concerning an Irish woman who travelled to England to have a pregnancy with a fatal foetal anomaly terminated) the committee again found that being forced to travel to access abortion care in the case of a foetal anomaly amounted to torture and ill-treatment as well as a violation of the right to privacy. The committee found discrimination on socioeconomic grounds but not gender.

It is important to emphasise that international treaties serve a key purpose in highlighting human rights standards and identifying breaches of standards; however, they cannot compel states to take action to redress discrimination and inequalities. It appears, though, that international treaty bodies are becoming more explicit in advocating for global abortion laws which allow for abortion in at least a minimum number of circumstances. There is also a clear understanding that a lack of access to abortion impacts on maternal mortality but also on women's physical and mental health. Going forward, it is evident that there is a growing understanding that women must have access to abortion under certain circumstances at a minimum. We return to this debate on the use of human rights to frame abortion access in the next chapter, with a consideration of its use within a reproductive justice approach.

CEDAW Optional Protocol

In 2000, CEDAW adopted the Optional Protocol. This allows for individuals to make a complaint to CEDAW or for CEDAW to conduct an inquiry into grave or systematic violations of the convention by a particular state. Complaints have considered issues such as forced sterilisation, domestic violence and parental leave. Four inquiries have been completed into the following issues: the murder and disappearances of Aboriginal women and girls in Canada; the abduction, rape and murder of women in Mexico; access to contraception; reproductive and sexual health in the Philippines (as detailed in the forthcoming section); and access to abortion in Northern Ireland. Each of the inquiries found evidence of the state failing to protect women and girls and recommended a range of actions to rectify this.

Commentators argue that while the aspirations of CEDAW are to be commended, its inability to enforce sanctions on those states who fail to meet standards is problematic (O'Rourke, 2016). Using Northern Ireland as a case study, O'Rourke (2016) illustrates how the UK as the state party has repeatedly ignored challenges from CEDAW that it has failed to address discrimination against women regarding access to abortion. This lack of action contrasts with the collaborative efforts of pro-choice organisations, who have lobbied for legal reform. These efforts culminated in a request for an Optional Protocol Inquiry, which was submitted to CEDAW in 2012. However, as O'Rourke notes, the efforts of the collaborators did not result in them securing the support of 'mainstream' human rights organisations in the jurisdiction. As Pierson and Bloomer (2017) highlight, the lack of engagement from these organisations results from a combination of factors, including anti-abortion stances held by senior staff and concerns about the impact on wider campaigns. In Northern Ireland the rights-based framework to abortion has not translated up to the macro political level where decision-making takes place. It is significant to note that several of these organisations met with the CEDAW investigation team when it conducted its inquiry in 2016, and that upon publication of the results in 2018, were supportive of its findings that grave and systematic human right violations had been identified in Northern Ireland, with respect to access to abortion (Bloomer et al, 2018b; CEDAW, 2018).

Has CEDAW been effective? Englehart and Miller (2014) determined that it was possible to consider the impact of CEDAW by utilising a series of quantitative indicators to assess women's political, social and economic rights. Their study of 149 countries found that CEDAW ratification was a significant predictor of women's political rights, and less so, but still visible, social rights, though not women's economic rights (Englehart and Miller, 2014: 27). The authors argue that while rights may exist, how they are exercised in practice may vary. This matter is explored by Liebowitz and Zwingel (2014), who posit that assessing the impact of CEDAW is challenging, due to difficulties in measurement. They argue that gender-related indices are limited to what can be quantified. In so doing, the end product often simplifies phenomena that are multilayered, complex and constituted through multiple forms of agency (Liebowitz and Zwingel, 2014: 363). Using Chile as a case study, the authors illustrate the contrast between quantitative measures and the CEDAW monitoring process, demonstrating that the latter is much more effective, as it allows for a combination of 'widely accepted women's rights standards, context-specificity, and a focus on process-oriented agency' (Liebowitz and Zwingel, 2014: 363). It is argued that the CEDAW process challenges the implied notion in quantitative monitoring that achieving gender equality is a race that can be won, as opposed to one that is fluid, dynamic and needs continual practice.

Case study: The Philippines

The Republic of the Philippines is situated in the western Pacific Ocean and consists of about 7,641 islands. The capital city is Manila and the most populous city is Quezon City; both form part of Metro Manila. The Philippines has a population of approximately 101 million. As of January 2018, it was the eighth most populated country in Asia and the twelfth most populated country in the world.

The Philippines has one of the largest populations of Catholics in the world. About eight in ten Filipinos (81%) are Roman Catholic. Because of its colonial history and continuing power, the Catholic Church exercises tremendous influence on the nation and the state (Pangalangan, 2015). Many Filipinos have conservative views on social issues in line with Catholic Church teachings. Two thirds (67%) state that getting a divorce is morally unacceptable and an overwhelming majority believe that having an abortion is immoral (93%). In citing these statistics, Pew Research Center (Lipka, 2015) notes that 'no country among the 40 surveyed is more universally opposed to abortion on moral grounds', stating further that, 'the Philippines consistently has displayed a "low" level of government restrictions on religion'.

The Philippines is classified as medium on the Human Development Index (HDI) and is ranked 114th out of 187 countries and territories (HDN, 2013). Yet 21.6% of the population live below the poverty line. Furthermore, large inequities exist. Farmers, fishermen and children belonging to families with income below the official poverty threshold posted the highest poverty indices at 34.3%, 34.0% and 31.4%, respectively. Women belonging to poor families had higher poverty incidence than the general population (PSA, 2017).

Approximately 25 million Philippine citizens are women of reproductive age. Levels of unintended pregnancy are high, largely as a result of relatively low levels of contraceptive use. Consequently, women resort to illegal and unsafe abortion, with high levels of mortality and morbidity. In 2000, the abortion rate was estimated as ranging between 22 and 31 abortions per 1,000 women of reproductive age. This rate is considerably higher than the unsafe abortion rate for Southeast Asia as a whole. It is estimated that 560,000 abortions took place in the Philippines in 2008, and 610,000 in 2012, based on the 2000 national abortion rate, and taking into account population increases. Further estimated data indicates that around 1,000 women and girls die annually as a result of unsafe abortion (Juarez et al, 2005; Guttmacher Institute, 2013). As demonstrated below, attempts to improve access to abortion have been extremely problematic.

In terms of the structure of governance, the Philippines Local Government code of 1991 introduced a major devolution of national government services. The code devolved basic services for agriculture extension, forest management, health services, barangay (township) roads and social welfare to Local Government Units. In 1992, the management and delivery of health services was devolved from the National Department of Health to locally elected provincial, city and municipal governments. This has allowed local officials to determine what kind of health services will be delivered to their constituents, despite the establishment of national standards.

In 2012, the UN Human Rights Committee, in its concluding observations on the fourth periodic review of the Philippines, expressed that it 'regrets the absolute ban on abortions, which compels pregnant women to seek clandestine and harmful abortion services, and accounts for a significant number of maternal deaths' (UNICCPR, 2012: 3). It called on the Philippine government to:

> review its legislation with a view to making provision for exceptions to the prohibition of abortion, such as protection of life or health of the mother, and pregnancy resulting from rape or incest, in order to prevent women from having to seek clandestine harmful abortions. (UNICCPR, 2012: 3)

Three years later, in 2015, the CEDAW Committee called on the Philippines:

> To amend articles 256 to 259 of its Criminal Code to legalize abortion in cases of rape, incest, threats to the life and/or health of the mother or serious malformation of the foetus and to decriminalize all other cases in which women undergo abortion, as well as to adopt the procedural rules necessary to guarantee effective access to legal abortion. (CEDAW, 2016: 15)

The following year, 2016, the CEDAW Committee's concluding observations on the combined seventh and eighth periodic reports of the Philippines referred to the 2015 recommendation, stating, 'That there has been a lack of specific measures to implement the recommendations of the Committee's inquiry conducted in 2015 (CEDAW/C/OP.8/PHL/1), including with regard to access to modern contraceptives and the legalization of abortion under certain circumstances' (CEDAW, 2016: 11).

The call for the revision of the Philippine's extremely restrictive laws, which practically ban abortion under all circumstances, follows on from earlier positions by various UN human rights bodies that absolute abortion bans violate the prohibition of torture and ill-treatment (UNCAT, 2006).

As stated earlier in this chapter, UN bodies have made such recommendations to other governments. What is different in the Philippines case is that all three documents make these recommendations in reference to Executive Order 003 (EO 003), 'Declaring Total Commitment and Support to the Responsible Parenthood Movement in the City of Manila and Enunciating Policy Declarations in Pursuit Thereof', propagated by the Mayor of Manila, Jose L. Atienza Jr, on 29 February 2000. EO 003 declared that Manila:

> promotes responsible parenthood and upholds natural family planning not just as a method but as a way of self-awareness in promoting the culture of life while discouraging the use of artificial methods of contraception like condoms, pills, intrauterine devices, surgical sterilization, and other.

While EO 003 did not call for an outright ban, its implementation led to the withdrawal for at least a decade of all modern contraceptive methods other than natural family planning in Manila. Its implementation resulted in the loss of medical supplies and services in city-run healthcare facilities, upon which many poor women depended. Nongovernmental organisations, which had supplemented Manila's reproductive health services and could have taken up some of the slack, were also closed down. Health worker employees of these NGOs were harassed. The ban led to the effective deprivation of contraceptives for poor women in Manila with negative impacts on their health and socioeconomic conditions (Demeterio-Melgar et al, 2007).

The context of the executive order's emphasis on natural family planning is important. As noted earlier, the Philippines is an overwhelmingly Catholic country. It is also the last bastion of Catholic conservatism in Asia. In 2000, when EO 003 was promulgated, the Philippines had already set out on a long road of debate around reproductive health including contraceptives. The Catholic Bishops' Conference in that same year (CBCP, 2000) had declared a 'prolife position' that opposed abortion and looked upon all modern contraceptives as anti-life and/ or abortifacient. The Church's only approved method of fertility control is what it calls 'natural family planning'.

Since the time of Spanish colonisation, politicians in the Philippines have curried favour with the Church. This has included taking strong stands against contraceptives since the early 1990s. Atienza's ban on contraception in Manila was by no means the only ban by local officials, with others instigated at different times and locations (Jimenez-David, 2011; CRR, 2015). Church pressure on all branches of government on the issues of abortion and contraception is a given in Philippine society. The Church established allies among powerful politicians, including Gloria Macapagal Arroyo, who for almost the entire period of the ban in Manila was President of the Philippines, despite being beset by a series of scandals. The most serious threat was a crisis in which there was credible evidence that she had cheated in order to win the presidency.

In the cases of former presidents Ferdinand Marcos (1966–86) and Joseph Estrada (1988–2001), the Church had been a factor in their ousting. In the case of Arroyo, the Church had proven to be her saviour (Rufo, 2013). During her administration, Arroyo and most of her allies in the legislature ensured the defeat of reproductive health bills. She also consistently de-emphasised and defunded reproductive health programmes in the country (Estrada Claudio, 2010a). Furthermore, despite constitutional guarantees of the separation of powers, it is widely held that the Philippine Executive can and does wield tremendous influence on the judiciary when it deems this politically necessary. Arroyo was also president for the majority of the period when the ban in Manila was challenged in the Philippine courts, a lengthy process which was later critiqued by the Center for Reproductive Rights (CRR, 2008, 2015).

In January 2008, 20 male and female residents from Manila's poor communities who had been denied access to the full range of contraceptive services and information, particularly modern methods of contraception such as condoms, pills and intrauterine devices, filed a petition before the Court of Appeals to obtain redress for violations of reproductive rights committed under EO 003. The petitioners filed for a temporary restraining order and/or writ of preliminary injunction to prevent the occurrence of new violations. The lead petitioner in the case, Lourdes Osil, had given birth to two children prior to the adoption of EO 003; after EO 003 went into effect, denying her contraceptive information and services, she ultimately had five more unplanned pregnancies. As documented in a 2007 research study (Demeterio-Melgar et al, 2007), Osil and the other petitioners had testified to the severe strain on their families as a result of the ban and the subsequent unwanted pregnancies which resulted. Rules of Civil Procedure mandate that the Court of Appeals act on this sort of petition within 24 hours. However, in May 2008 the case was dismissed without a hearing, and a motion for reconsideration was denied in August 2008 (CRR, 2008). The Court of Appeals justified this dismissal by the absence of 'tax declarations' from the petitioners as a means of proving that they were indeed indigents. The court also stated that the case should have been filed before the Regional Trial Court of Manila (RTC), a body with concurrent jurisdiction with the Court of Appeals

(CRR, 2008). The petitioners in the case Osil v. Office of the Mayor of the City of Manila then appealed to the Supreme Court, which dismissed their case in October 2008 on the grounds that one of the petitioners had failed to sign the petition. The Supreme Court did not rule on the merits of the case regarding the 19 petitioners who had signed the petition. A motion for reconsideration was denied in December 2008. In April 2009, the case was refiled before the RTC. After almost three years, a motion to dismiss filed by the City of Manila before the RTC was denied. A second motion to dismiss was, however, granted in October 2014. The petition was dismissed on the grounds that it had become moot and academic because of the passage of the national reproductive health law which allowed for reproductive health and family planning services, though abortion remained illegal (CRR, 2015).

As reproductive health advocates began to despair of the processes of justice within the Philippines, UN mechanisms for redress were invoked. On 2 June 2008, CEDAW received a joint submission from three nongovernmental organisations requesting that it conduct an inquiry under article 8 of the Optional Protocol to CEDAW into EO 003. Updated information was submitted in April 2009, July 2010 and April 2012. The updated information alleged that the executive order continued to be implemented under the subsequent mayor, Alfredo Lim, elected in 2007, who had issued a new executive order (EO 030), which had imposed a funding ban on modern contraception (CEDAW, 2015).

The case was only the second inquiry conducted under Article 8 of the Optional Protocol to CEDAW and the first on sexual and reproductive health rights (ESCR-Net, 2015). After a review of the information and upon receiving a reply from the Philippine government that denied all allegations, a confidential inquiry was conducted by the CEDAW Committee that included a visit by two of its members to the Philippines in November 2012. The outcome of the inquiry was published in April 2015, with the CEDAW Committee, acting within the mandate of Protocol II, stating that it found the Philippine government accountable for grave and systematic violations of women's rights. In its report, the CEDAW Committee took pains to establish that despite the devolution of authority to the local officials of Manila, the national government had failed to protect women's rights by its lack of monitoring and accountability mechanisms to hold local authorities to national standards.

While celebrated as a victory by women's rights advocates, the CEDAW Committee's decision also presented challenges. First, by the time of the release of the committee's findings the Philippines had a new president, Benigno Simeon C. Aquino III, who had expended large amounts of political capital to ensure the passage of the reproductive health legislation which he signed into law in

December 2012. It seemed ironic to the government officials under the Aquino administration that they would be held accountable for violations committed by previous authorities at the local and national government level. Second, although contraceptive access had begun to improve by the time of the release of the CEDAW Committee's findings, access continued to be below standard (PopCom, 2017). Third, despite both the CEDAW report and the passage of the reproductive health law, the Church and its allies continued to place barriers to contraceptive access. For example, Church-based groups managed to secure yet another temporary restraining order on certain contraceptives in August 2014 (Supreme Court, 2014). This was later overturned in November 2017 and yet another mayor has now banned contraceptives in her city using the same 'pro-life' rhetoric of EO 003 (Office of the Mayor, Sorsogon City, 2015). Of note, however, is that this case is expected to be challenged by the Department of Health (Geronimo, 2016).

If the struggle for contraceptive access is so fraught in the Philippines, it is little wonder that despite repeated episodes of censure and pressure by the international community, the total ban on abortion remains firmly in place. With little sign of improved access to abortion, activists and health professionals have focused their efforts to improve access to post-abortion care, in an attempt to reduce mortality rates from unsafe abortion.

International humanitarian intervention

A record number of people around the world are currently facing displacement due to conflict and persecution – 65 million in 2015 – half of whom are women and girls (Guttmacher Institute, 2017a). Those forced from their homes are caught in humanitarian and crisis situations encompassing a range of human-made and natural emergencies, including armed conflict, political instability, natural disasters, epidemics and famine – which are often multiplied and compounded. Those from poor and fragile states with limited ability to carry out basic governance functions are even more prone to the effects of disasters and crises. While women and girls experience many of the same harms as men and boys in conflict and crisis, they also have sexual and reproductive health needs which are often unmet in, and exacerbated by, crisis situations. Safe access to abortion and post-abortion care are included within these needs.

Until about 20 years ago, global awareness of and responsiveness to women's sexual and reproductive health and rights during a conflict or crisis were largely lacking. Instead, humanitarian responses made access to food, water, shelter, sanitation and immediate medical assistance the priorities. In 1994, a seminal report by the organisation now known as the Women's Refugee Commission outlined the case for prioritising the reproductive health of women in crisis (Wulf, 1994). Following this, UN conferences on women's health and rights in Cairo in 1994 and Beijing in 1995 recognised that women displaced by a conflict or crisis have the same right to reproductive health as all women. In 1995, a consortium of nongovernmental organisations (NGOs), donors, governments and UN agencies created the Inter-Agency Working Group on Reproductive Health in Crisis (IAWG), which has since grown to over 2,100 individual members and 450 agencies. The group produced a manual to provide guidance to field staff on reproductive health interventions during emergencies. This was updated in 2010 to include a new chapter on safe abortion care and post-abortion care, addressing a gap in the original document.

Work on gender and development has made clear that conflict and crisis affects women's access to reproductive health, and increases in unsafe abortion are widely reported by those working in the field (Busza and Lush, 1999). Literature has particularly noted the effects of conflict on displaced women (Palmer and Zwi, 1999), including a steady increase in both births and abortions in refugee camps, the prohibition of contraceptive and abortion services by religious relief organisations (Wulf, 1994), and displacement affecting women's desired family size (Palmer and Zwi, 1999). Although literature and policy recognise the unique vulnerabilities of women and girls, and guidelines have been developed to address their needs, the sexual and reproductive health needs of women and girls continue to go unmet during emergencies. Studies on specific services, such as family planning, highlight that while efforts have been made to improve access to contraception, including emergency contraception, in refugee camp settings, multiple barriers are experienced. These include 'distant service delivery points, cost of transport, lack of knowledge about different types of methods, misinformation and misconceptions, religious opposition, cultural factors, language barriers with providers, and provider biases' (Tanabe et al, 2017: 9). A new initiative, launched in June 2018 by Ipas, specifically set out to address this last point on provider biases, having identified that attention needed to be addressed to negative attitudes and fears related to providing abortion amongst humanitarian professionals (Ipas, 2018). Such initiatives are, however, set within a context of flaws at international policy levels.

One example of the weakness at policy level is the UN's development of policy with regard to gender and conflict: the Women, Peace and

Security Resolutions. The resolutions, developed since the initial Resolution 1325 in 2000, have recognised the underrepresentation of women in conflict mediation and peace-building but also the prevalence and impact of sexual violence in conflict. Despite the focus on sexual violence and its redress, the resolutions make little mention of sexual and reproductive health (Thomson and Pierson, 2018). Only Resolution 2106 (passed in 2013) contains an explicit reference to reproductive rights. Importantly, the resolution is framed in the language of 'health' rather than rights, with no greater specificity as to what the resolution might actually refer to in terms of service provision:

> Recognizing the importance of providing timely assistance to survivors of sexual violence, urges United Nations entities and donors to provide non-discriminatory and comprehensive health services, including sexual and reproductive health, psychosocial, legal, and livelihood support and other multi-sectoral services for survivors of sexual violence, taking into account the specific needs of persons with disabilities.

This is an important consideration. Policy developed at the international level is fundamentally a compromise between states. It is the result of complex negotiations centred on varied and competing interests between state parties, many of whom have very different national laws and policies on abortion. The controversial nature of abortion means that international cooperation and agreement will always prove difficult, and lack of commitment will filter into funding and services on the ground.

An evaluation undertaken by Inter Agency Working Group on Reproductive Health in Crisis in 2015 found that safe abortion care is a particular deficiency in sexual and reproductive health care in crisis (IAWG, 2015). The Guttmacher Institute (2017a) suggests that services are lacking for four key reasons:

- Cultural norms and ideological opposition to family planning and abortion, among other matters, often impede access to services, both before and during a crisis.
- Insufficient data makes it difficult to quantify the need for care, and to design and evaluate evidence-based interventions.

- Financial shortfalls lead to chronic underfunding of reproductive health care, particularly in areas like safe abortion and family planning.
- Weak overall health systems, which have often already deprioritised reproductive health, are easily overwhelmed by a crisis and unable to recover quickly.

Countries such as Sweden are beginning to promote a new approach to foreign policymaking with, for instance, an action plan and handbook for a feminist foreign policy. Two focus areas of the action plan are to 'Strengthen the human rights of women and girls in humanitarian settings' and to 'Strengthen the sexual and reproductive rights of girls and young people' (Government Offices of Sweden, 2015, 2018). The UK's Department for International Development also has a progressive policy with regard to abortion access provision, stating that the UK's 'position is that safe abortion reduces recourse to unsafe abortion and thus saves lives, and that women and adolescent girls must have the right to make their own decisions about their sexual and reproductive health and well-being' (DFID, 2013). The approaches of individual countries' foreign policy towards women's reproductive rights are beginning to create a stronger framework to ensure that such rights are protected even in crisis and that services remain available.

However, despite some progressive foreign policy, one of the most regressive policies hampering women's access to abortion and reproductive health more broadly has come from the US. The Mexico City policy (commonly referred to as the 'Global Gag Rule', originally imposed by Ronald Reagan in 1984 and subsequently lifted and re-imposed by Democrat and Republican presidents respectively) was reinstated by the US President Donald Trump as the first executive order of his presidency. The policy removes funding from any organisation that 'performs or actively promotes abortion as a method of family planning' overseas. Specifically, it removes funding from the following:

- Foreign NGOs that perform abortions or acknowledge abortion as a family planning option will be cut off from US funding and technical assistance.
- Foreign NGOs that perform abortions or acknowledge abortion as a family planning option will not be eligible to receive sub-grants from organisations based in the US or foreign NGOs that sign the

Global Gag Rule. They will also not be eligible to receive non-US global health funds through partnerships or consortiums with non-US based NGOs and NGOs that sign the Global Gag Rule, which includes receiving reproductive health supplies from those organisations.

• Health workers at foreign NGOs receiving US funding are barred from counselling women on abortion as an option for terminating their pregnancies, and from referring women to an abortion provider.

However, Trump has gone further and applied the policy to any organisation that receives funding from USAid, not just those involved in family planning. This decision has huge implications for the funding of reproductive health in development work and for abortion access in particular, both in crisis situations and beyond. IPPF highlights examples of the effect of the Global Gag Rule: in 2003, the Family Guidance Association of Ethiopia (FGAE), an IPPF Member Association, had to stop offering free condoms at its clinics due to recurring shortages. FGAE's Nazareth branch warned of an upcoming shortage of the Depo-Provera injectable, the contraceptive method used by 70% of its clients (IPPF, 2017).

The context within which reproductive and sexual health services are provided in crisis situations is, as detailed above, one where commitment to safe abortion care is particularly problematic. Commitments at both the international and the national level are difficult to guarantee, and reductions in funding impact on those who are most vulnerable. It is within this context that the IPPF has created its humanitarian crisis unit.

Case Study: The IPPF Humanitarian Unit

We have to be angry, we have to be bold. (Interview with IPPF, 2018)

The International Planned Parenthood Federation (IPPF) was set up during the third International Conference on Planned Parenthood in 1952. It initially comprised eight national family planning associations. Currently the charity is a federation of 142 Member Associations working in 153 countries, with another 23 Partners working in 18 countries. In 2016, IPPF and partners delivered 182.5 million sexual and reproductive health services worldwide. The federation has a central office in London and six regional offices in Nairobi, Tunis, Bangkok (two offices), Brussels and New York.

IPPF works on providing sexual and reproductive health services, but also on advocacy and campaigning both internationally and regionally, and on educational and awareness-raising programmes. IPPF's strategy is to ensure that by 2022:

- 100 governments respect, protect and fulfil sexual and reproductive rights.
- One billion people act freely on their sexual and reproductive health rights and needs.
- IPPF and its partners deliver two billion sexual and reproductive health services.
- IPPF will become a united Federation.

In an interview with an IPPF Director of Programmes, it was acknowledged that opposition to abortion services has become more visible in the past five years due to movements in the Global North which oppose abortion rights and challenges to service delivery in the Global South. This is compounded by the Global Gag Rule mentioned above. In response to the Global Gag Rule, IPPF hosts a Safe Abortion Action Fund (SAAF) to support global abortion-related programmes. Set up in 2006 and funded by the UK, Danish, Norwegian, Swedish and Swiss governments, it provides small grants to locally run organisations that promote safe abortion through advocacy and awareness training, service delivery and research. By the end of 2016, SAAF had provided over US$43 million of funding to 88 projects in over 62 countries.

Recognition of the effect of conflict on women's reproductive and sexual health needs led IPPF to set up a humanitarian crisis unit in 2007: SPRINT: Sexual and reproductive health in crisis and post-crisis situations. This was in order to address the gaps in the Minimum Initial Service Package (MISP), which outlines the minimum standard of reproductive health care in crisis settings. This unit is supported by the Australian Government, and since 2007 it has supported circa 890,000 people in over 62 emergency situations – 77% of the people it helps are women.

An example of the work that IPPF does and the support it offers can be seen in the Syrian conflict. Since 2011, more than half a million people have been killed in Syria and more than 10 million have fled their homes. One of IPPF's partner organisations, the Syrian Family Planning Association, is based in Aleppo, Syria's largest city. It has continued to provide services throughout the conflict, including services from mobile clinics, delivering contraceptive supplies and essential medicines and vitamins. The association's director, Dr Lama Mouakea, notes that sexual violence is a high risk for women and girls in the conflict, and psychological as well as practical help must be provided for those affected (IPPF, 2016).

Another setting where IPPF has provided services is Nepal. In 2015, Nepal suffered a major earthquake causing massive devastation and loss of life. It was the worst natural disaster to strike the country for 80 years – and one the country is still recovering from. Three million people were displaced, 22,000 were injured and 9,000 people lost their lives. The cost of damage, loss and reconstruction is estimated to be $14.6 billion – around three quarters of the country's entire gross domestic product for 2015. The earthquake and its aftermath had severe effects on healthcare and family planning. Clinics and hospitals were destroyed and those facilities that survived quickly became overcrowded. Millions of people were forced from their homes into tents, often many miles from their usual clinics and family planning centres. Women, girls and orphans were particularly vulnerable and were exposed to sexual violence. IPPF's partner (the Family Planning Association Nepal) offered essential items like oral rehydration solutions, medicines, food and water. It also distributed contraception and dignity kits, provided women with antenatal checks, and set up blood-testing labs and psychosocial counselling services. Women- and child-friendly spaces were created in order for the most vulnerable to be safe. The organisation also organised classes on menstrual hygiene and taught women and girls how to make sanitary pads from scratch.

Conclusions

Sexual and reproductive health rights and services have been marginal both in international human rights law and within crisis interventions by the international community. Since the late 1990s, the attention drawn to these issues, both through feminist academic scholarship and through activism, has meant that these issues have become more visible on the international stage. Abortion is the most controversial aspect of sexual and reproductive health, with the most widespread and varied legal positions taken by states. Consequently, arguing for legal change through a rights–based framework, or for funding in crisis situations specifically for abortion or abortion care, remains a difficult issue. However, the developments that have occurred in this arena in the last 20 years indicate that progress is being made and that abortion as a right and a healthcare service, while still controversial, is beginning to be recognised as a key issue for gender equality and crisis healthcare.

SIX

Activism

Within countries where abortion is restricted or under threat, groups have organised on an international, regional and local basis to lobby governments and campaign for women's right to safe and legal abortion, as well as seeking ways to work within, and where necessary circumvent, the law, to provide access to abortion. This chapter offers insight into a number of highly successful organisations such as Women Help Women, inroads, Abortion Support Network, the International Campaign for Women's Right to Safe Abortion and Amnesty International. The breadth of activism around the world could indeed warrant the attention of a publication in itself. We have in this chapter selected exemplars of organisations that operate on a transnational basis, who collaborate with grassroots movements, encouraging shared learning and knowledge across disciplines. As noted in other chapters which feature the work of activist organisations such as IPPF (Chapter Five), Women on Web (Chapters Two and Three) and RESURJ (Chapter Seven), the role of activist organisations is key to understanding abortion politics.

There is a richness of evidence on twentieth-century activism, with a growing body of analysis of more recent trends. For instance, the advancement of new technologies has improved information-sharing within and between countries and campaigns, through global listserves, social media and other platforms. Developments in telemedicine have led to improvements in access, as demonstrated in Chapter Two on, 'Criminalisation', and Chapter Three, 'Biomedicalisation'. This chapter will consider organisations who provide abortions outside of legal frameworks, those who work to fund abortions, those who campaign for improved access and those who focus on grassroots activism. It includes an examination of organisations which have not been subject to previous analysis and considers cross-movement solidarities that have emerged in the twenty-first century.

Overcoming barriers to accessing abortion may take individualised forms, such as seeking abortion away from legal settings, or collective forms. A spectrum exists of what is considered resistance, ranging from deliberate non-action to subtle and also more deliberate/blatant forms (Mishtal, 2016). For instance, a health worker may ignore evidence that a colleague has performed an abortion and that they recorded it as another procedure; another might provide information on alternative providers and direct an abortion seeker to reputable providers of abortion medication. The resistance may be actioned by those directly affected or by intermediaries. Often it is most visible when the resistance forms contentious politics. As feminist philosopher Alison Jaggar argues, when shared reality biases are held firmly by the powerful, contentious politics are often necessary to induce large numbers of people to re-examine deeply entrenched norms. Social movements are one method for waging contentious politics, providing a powerful social practice for the peaceful transformation of moral consciousness, and undermining the moral authority of those in power (Anderson, 2014; Jaggar, 2014). Biased moral thinking has frequently been challenged by social movements, operating on national and transnationals levels. Their goals have been to provide alternatives to dominant ways of thinking and to pressure the powerful into taking those arguments seriously. The battle to overcome restrictive laws and to challenge abortion stigma often means undermining the moral authority of governments, of churches, the fiercely held values of anti-abortion lobbying organisations and misogyny institutionalised in healthcare.

It is evident that activists have played a pivotal role in advocating for access to safe abortion and the broader asks of reproductive justice. Activists have emerged from a range of fields and social movement allies, including community, health, academic, political, artistic, legal, trade union, students' union, and human rights law and activism. Many of those involved in abortion rights activism may not have been politically active previously. Activists may have been drawn to involvement following their awareness of an issue in the media or having been directly affected:

> 'I think it is important we recognise that some of our most powerful activists are just normal people who read a news story or had a personal experience or knew someone who had a personal experience and started standing on the barricades.' (Mara Clarke, Abortion Support Network, interview, 2018)

Their work includes one or more of the following activities: providing abortions, funding abortions and associated costs, education/stigma-busting, knowledge creation and information dissemination, lobbying, research, training, legal challenges, and protests/awareness-raising. Contemporary activism has benefited greatly from technological advances. Social media-based activism is often characterised as superficial or 'hashtag activism', but such dismissal fails to recognise the tangible benefits that come from utilising online spaces. For those advocating for abortion access, there is the potential to engage in solidarity actions globally, the potential for telemedicine to provide direct help to women who need to access abortion while living under restrictive regimes, the ability to connect with those who may not feel comfortable making their activism public, the space to share successful strategies and knowledge, and most importantly, the space to share abortion stories and experiences. Transnational feminism enables us to witness the global nature of control of women's reproductive lives and often the similar forms this takes. A transnational approach provides a global solidarity movement, yet it must also be situated in local contexts. Attempts to convey the global nature of women's reproductive oppression, though vitally important, must not override the need to interrogate the specific circumstances under which this occurs, otherwise there is the chance that intersectionality will be lost.

In the chapter detailing the criminalisation of abortion (Chapter Two), we noted that those performing abortions have included women in the community who have also fulfilled the role of midwives, doctors, vets, pharmacists, herbalists, lay health practitioners and masseurs (McLaren, 1978). In this chapter, we shall begin by considering the more recent history of activists who have provided abortions outside of the legal framework. This is followed by a series of case studies of organisations and collectives operating in the twenty-first century, who work within specific geographic areas and also transnationally. This chapter illuminates the work of activists working in different ways, from those who are involved in direct activism (service provision) to those who work on longer-term strategic activism to change laws and social attitudes towards abortion.

Abortion providers

Beginning in 1969, the Jane collective, also known as the Service, operated in Chicago, US, firstly as an information and counselling service for women seeking abortions, before moving to providing abortions in 1971. Between 1969 and 1973 it is estimated that they provided/facilitated access to 11,000 abortions (Bart, 1987; Kaplan, 1997). Women were charged a fee of $50 dollars, which was only paid if the woman could afford it. Knowledge about the service was provided through organisations such as the Chicago Women's Liberation Union or shared among personal connections. Referrals to the service also came from law enforcement, who, it appears, largely adopted a position of non-interference with the service. Bart (1987) argues that this was because police officers personally knew women who had used the service, had used the service themselves, and/or viewed the collective as providing safe access to abortion compared to other backstreet providers. This discretion on the part of the police worked well, and on only one occasion was an investigation conducted, after a new police captain had been appointed who was unaware of the informal arrangements. While Jane volunteers were arrested in this instance, the charges were quickly dropped.

The Jane service operated from private locations, to which the woman would be taken after arriving at a meeting place, in order to minimise exposure. Counselling was offered in one-to-one or group settings, with group settings favoured, as it allowed those seeking abortion to provide support to each other. The purpose of the counselling was to demystify the abortion process. Follow-up checks were conducted and advice offered on birth control (Kaplan, 1997).

Some of those involved in Jane had come from feminist backgrounds. For others the growing political changes, in the context of anti-war protests in the late 1960s and high-profile instances of police brutality, had led to politicisation. Many had originally joined a feminist organisation, the Women's Liberation Union, seeking opportunities to do something for and with women (Kaplan, 1997). The move to become abortion providers came after activists learned that the man they were referring women to for abortions was not a qualified clinician. The women involved in Jane therefore acquired the necessary skills and began providing abortions themselves. The surplus money, which no longer needed to be paid to the abortion provider, was used to provide financial support to volunteers, many of whom were not in employment, or could only access low-paid jobs.

Those involved in the Jane collective expressed high levels of satisfaction with their volunteering, and they linked this to recognising that what they did was of immediate help to the women using their services. Bart (1987) argues that others forms of activism could not deliver this sense of satisfaction: those working in rape crisis centres or domestic violence shelters could not undo the violence; they could assist with support and recovery. In contrast, the Jane collective could offer concrete help. In addition, the women developed skills in dealing with health issues, making referrals, counselling and abortion provision. Collectively they learned a great deal and did so within a supportive environment. The care provided was woman-centred, with some commenting that it was of significantly better quality than support they had accessed in legal settings in later years. This was largely ascribed to the fact that Jane was grounded in women's experiences. The collective nature of the organisation, minimal hierarchy, and how easy it in fact was to provide a safe abortion, all served to build cohesion and sharing of skills:

> To use Ehrenreich and English's phrase (1973), these women seized the 'technology without buying the ideology'; that is, they used antibiotics and medical equipment but did not adopt the hierarchical system or the sense of entitlement that characterizes physicians. (Bart, 1987: 355)

The Jane collective has come under renewed interest in recent years in the US, with consistent and increasing anti-abortion regulations leading to discussions of the need for new Jane collectives. The release in the US (in 2018) of two feature films on the work of the Jane collective illustrates contemporary interest in resistance to restricted abortion access.

The Jane collective is a well-known and oft-cited example of abortion provision in situations which are illegal. Its iconic status among activists working in the area is well-deserved recognition of pioneering work done in dangerous circumstances. But it is also worthy of consideration because many groups continue to provide abortions in situations where these are illegal and at great risk to themselves whilst having to remain hidden. Obviously, these groups cannot be identified. Abortion provision in illegal circumstances has existed across historical periods and continues to exist today in all countries where restrictions exist. Indeed, the documentation of the high rates of maternal mortality and morbidity has been a continuing project of cooperation between academia and abortion activists since the beginnings of the women's health movement in the late 1970s (Estrada–Claudio, 2010b). That documentation has been used in several ways: to challenge the idea that abortions can be banned in the first place; to establish abortion as a need that women will always fulfil regardless of barriers; to call attention to the reasons women risk their lives to get an abortion, thus arguing that it is a human right that allows women to live in dignity; to argue for the legalisation of abortions.

A distinction needs to be made, however, between activist providers and other forms of illegal providers. Both types of abortion providers exist where abortion is illegal, as discussed in Chapters Two and Three. But the motivations for service provision are very different and may therefore lead to very different outcomes. While not all abortion providers in illegal contexts use unsafe methods, a large number do. It is also likely that non-activists who perform illegal but safe abortions charge a high fee, putting their services out of reach of women in lower socioeconomic groups. However, quality of service issues, other than mortality and morbidity concerns, mark out activist service provision in these settings. These considerations include ensuring proper clinical protocols, keeping costs affordable, preventing judgment and stigmatisation, ensuring respectful provider/client relationships, ensuring proper information is given, and ensuring continuing care post abortion. Activist providers also carry security concerns beyond their own self-protection, and put in place adequate protocols that teach women how to deal with health and police authorities should they need to seek secondary or tertiary care for complications. The positioning of 'unsafe abortion' is thus complicated (Solinger, 1996; Joffe, 1996; 2009).

Support systems such as continuing education and upgrading of skills, as well as psychosocial care for activist providers in illegal contexts, are also necessary. Activist clinics must also look into the procurement of abortion supplies, whether these are misoprostol and mifepristone for medical abortions or supplies for other methods. Given the inherent difficulties that illegal providers face in their own state, the role of transnational networks cannot be discounted. These groups and networks provide training for providers, supplies, support and solidarity, as well as opportunities to share experiences. Given that legal contexts vary, transnational and international solidarity are able to leverage these differences, ensuring training, sharing speak-outs and other forms of support workshops during international conferences.

Illegal but legal

Activists have been confronting legal barriers in so many creative ways that it would be impossible to catalogue the various methods by which it can be done. A classic example is the case of Bangladesh (Dixon-Mueller, 1988). Under Bangladesh's penal code of 1860, induced abortion is illegal except to save a woman's life. However, in 1979 activists managed to position menstrual regulation as part of the National Family Planning Programme, 'to regulate the menstrual cycle when menstruation is absent for a short duration' (Guttmacher Institute, 2017b: 1). Today, menstrual regulation procedures include manual vacuum aspiration or a combination of mifepristone and misoprostol. The rules allow menstrual regulation procedures up to 10–12 weeks after a woman's last menstrual period, though medical menstrual regulation is allowed only up to nine weeks (Guttmacher Institute, 2017b). The legalisation of menstrual regulation and the subsequent fight to keep it accessible and safe, including its expansion to include medical abortion, is yet another interesting illustration of the many ways by which activists deal with legal restrictions.

Activists enabling self-managed abortion

Women Help Women was established as an international organisation in 2014 by a small group of feminist activists, who recruited health professionals and researchers to join them in their work. Its focus is to put abortion pills directly into women's hands, which it does via a telemedicine service, by building partnerships in restricted settings around the world with local activist groups who can support women in their own communities. It also works to shift the dialogue around abortion with pills. Women Help Women challenges the overmedicalised model of abortion provision, and works to document the efficacy and safety of self-managed abortion. As discussed in Chapter Three, Women Help Women activists initially prioritised developing strong partnerships in settings where telemedicine was problematic. Typically these were countries where packages of the medication were not being received at their intended destinations. The organisation sought to develop innovative means of providing access to the medication in such circumstances, with initial areas including the Republic of Ireland, Northern Ireland, Brazil and Poland. Within a three-year period the organisation had expanded to working in 40 countries across four continents.

In focusing on building relationships in the targeted countries, Women Help Women activists sought to build the capacity of small partner organisations by assisting them with funding plans, providing organisational and technical assistance, building alliances between groups to create national and regional networks, and enabling leadership-building in each setting. This progress has occurred in the face of a series of challenges: cybersecurity, misinformation and stigma. The need to maintain secure communications, with staff based on four continents and working in legally restricted settings, presents complex challenges. Monitoring of human rights activists is prevalent; thus secure communication is needed both to support teams and to provide services. The second key challenge faced by Women Help Women is tackling the deliberate misinformation and myths perpetuated about abortion. These range from innocent but harmful folklore to scare tactics that are dangerous. Typically these take the form of false information about the impact of abortion on physical and mental health. The third main challenge faced by Women Help Women is abortion stigma:

> 'In too many cultures having sex is stigmatised; having an abortion is a declaration that you have had sex, that you have completed the 'dirty deed'. The discourse too is littered with language about responsibility, accusations that the person should have taken contraception, with no acknowledgement that contraceptions are not foolproof ... The stigma about abortion is more enhanced in settings where abortion is restricted ... which is why so many opt to self-manage abortion in secrecy. It would be wonderful for these settings to move to a position on abortion that is similar to how we talk about periods, an everyday occurrence; we don't shout about it, but we recognise it is an everyday thing.' (Interview with Women Help Women activist, 2018)

It is noteworthy that these challenges are common to many activist organisations.

In terms of what lies ahead, Women Help Women activists are positive about the opportunities that abortion medication presents:

> 'It is safe, effective, inexpensive to produce. More and more studies provide clear evidence that it can be used to self-manage abortions; clinicians are changing their practice to adapt to this. As we raise awareness of the medications, this will help more and more of those who seek abortion in restricted settings. With the launch of an information project in the US in 2017, Women Help Women is directly challenging the medicalisation of and restricted access to abortion pills.' (Interview with Women Help Women activist, 2018)

As an organisation, Women Help Women seeks to move forward, strengthening existing partnerships and adding new partnerships, with the overarching goal of improving access to abortion for those in most need:

> 'The law is the law, and access is access. We are aware of those experiencing particular difficulties, in all types of

settings, the undocumented amongst others, for whom access is almost impossible. We will work with partners to reach these women.' (Interview with Women Help Women activist, 2018)

It is evident that the significant efforts of Women Help Women are enabling access to abortion for those in restricted settings, providing a safe way of terminating a pregnancy in medical terms. However, those choosing these methods are risking criminality in doing so. The existence of Women Help Women and other organisations are at present providing short-term solutions to endemic problems associated with access to abortion.

Abortion funders

Recognising that many women experience financial barriers to abortion, activists have sought to provide financial support to enable access. This typically includes full or part costs for the abortion procedure, travel costs and either costs for accommodation or providing access to hosts who offer accommodation in their homes. A contemporary example of an abortion funder is Abortion Support Network, a charity based in London that was set up in late 2009 by Mara Clarke. The Abortion Support Network is a contemporary example of support provided to women from Ireland, north and south, accessing abortion in England which mirrors the support of previous organisations that existed since the 1967 Abortion Act, including the London-based Irish Women's Abortion Support Group (1980–2000) and the Liverpool-based Liverpool Abortion Support Service (1981– 84) and Escort (1989–2006).

Abortion Support Network was founded on the understanding that making abortion against the law doesn't stop abortion but only stops safe abortion. It is not a campaigning or lobbying organisation. Instead, it positions itself as providing immediate, practical support to women and pregnant people who are unable to access safe and legal abortion in their own countries. The organisation was set up to mirror the work of American abortion funders associated with the National Network of Abortion Funds (NNAF), which Clarke had first encountered while living in the US. NNAF organisations seek to remove financial and logistical barriers to abortion access. In addition to costs and accommodation, some offer support such as transportation, childcare, translation and doula services.* Like NNAF organisations, Abortion Support Network also works with abortion providers to offer reduced abortion costs.

Abortion Support Network's primary purpose is to alleviate financial hardship for women forced to travel from home and pay for private abortions in England or occasionally further afield in Europe. Its client base is drawn primarily from the Republic of Ireland and Northern Ireland, with the Isle of Man and Channel Islands (regions of the British Isles where abortion is also restricted) a very distant third and fourth. It also offers information on abortion services (though not counselling), including information on reliable providers of abortion medication for those who wish to self-manage their abortion. The cost of accessing a private abortion in England ranges from £400 to £2,000 depending on the stage of the pregnancy. Abortion Support Network provides partial and full costs to those in dire financial circumstances, or those without access to the necessary funds within the timeframe that termination of pregnancy requires. Support may also include travel costs, and if needed accommodation costs. In some areas Abortion Support Network volunteer hosts provide accommodation and can accompany a woman to her clinic appointment. During the period 2009–17, the network provided funding to 1,088 clients, dealt with 4,185 cases/calls and hosted 182 clients. It raises funds through individual donations, sponsorship and fundraising activities. Its volunteers provide advice to women/girls of all ages, some of whom face a raft of barriers to accessing abortion, including visa issues, homelessness, domestic abuse, sexual crime and mental health problems. Donations and grant income have allowed the Abortion Support Network to meet the increased demand for its services. Mara Clarke, its founder and CEO, notes that while the increased income is to be welcomed, the constant challenges the organisation faces are worrying:

> 'We worry that funding will dry up, that policy changes are unclear, that even if legal change does occur, eg. in the Republic of Ireland, will the service be free? If not then we will still be needed. The impact of Brexit on travelling is unknown; travel for the undocumented is very difficult. The lack of information on how to access abortion is

---

* A doula is traditionally associated with the birthing process. They act in the role of companion, providing physical assistance and emotional support during and after the birth. Abortion doulas operate in some settings, particularly where abortion is restricted.

problematic, as too is the lack of unbiased information. Stigma and misinformation are rampant.' (Interview with Mara Clarke, Abortion Support Network, 2018)

The challenges for Abortion Support Network, many of which are common to those faced by Women Help Women, also present some opportunities, as Clarke acknowledges. For instance, a proposal for free access to abortion for those who travel to the rest of the UK from Northern Ireland was unclear in its rollout but has provided opportunities to increase awareness about the disparities in access in the UK. It also serves to highlight that even if financial barriers are removed, having to travel is a barrier in of itself for those who have caring responsibilities, are in a situation of domestic abuse and/or have other health concerns. "I am quietly hopeful. It does feel like change is ahead in Ireland, Northern Ireland and Isle of Man. The international attention from human rights organisations has helped; momentum is building" (interview with Mara Clarke, Abortion Support Network, 2018).

Clarke acknowledges that if the need for its services in current areas decreases, the organisation's primary focus will remain as removing financial barriers to abortion. Her hope is that Abortion Support Network's focus will shift to problematic access elsewhere in Europe. This is likely to include a focus on second trimester abortions, which are restricted in several European countries, as well as the protection of refugees seeking abortion and those without access to state systems. Core to this will be the organisation's continued focus on providing practical help. It studiously avoids lobbying – unlike NNAF, which it was modelled on – but is happy to work to raise the profile of those most affected, as well as the profile of the organisations campaigning for legal reform: "We are the plaster; the campaigning organisations are the cure." The organisation is supportive of the trend to self-manage abortions: "we support the philosophy of sisters doing it for themselves ... if the government can't take care of us then we will do it for ourselves, but we are also cautious about romanticising the abortion pill; it is not for everyone" (interview with Mara Clarke, Abortion Support Network, 2018).

Challenging abortion stigma

The International Network for the Reduction of Abortion Discrimination and Stigma (inroads) is a global network of advocates, scholars, health providers and donors interested in programme design, research and advocacy to address abortion stigma and its negative outcomes. Its reach extends to more than 79 countries, with over 900 members. The aim of the organisation is to end abortion stigma, so that abortion will be seen as normal and necessary. The organisation is grounded in a community of practice perspective, whereby members share knowledge, skills and learn from each other. There are four pillars of action: first, counteracting abortion stigma, raising awareness, considering the quality of care in reproductive health communities and focusing on the impact of abortion on the wellbeing of those affected; second, catalysing and supporting capacity-building – and identifying mechanisms to enable this; third, facilitating the generation of evidence, incorporating stigma reduction in programmes, amplifying research and supporting new research; fourth, gathering and connecting members, both online and in the real world, in face-to-face engagements. The demand for engagement is significant: membership has been through a period of rapid growth, doubling in size in 2016 alone (from 375 members to 875). Such growth presents particular challenges in meeting demand and finding resources to support members. This is all within a context of global challenges arising from the combined effect of the US's Global Gag Rule (detailed in Chapter Five) and the increase in traditional nationalist, right-wing movements, typified by organisations steeped in misogyny and pronatalist policies:

> These movements adopt a particular definition of equality; they attempt to use our language against us. At any one time someone in the network will be experiencing opposition from such organisations. Thankfully there will be others in the network who have energy to support them through that. (Interview with Katie Gillum, inroads co-convenor, 2018)

These challenges impact on the ability to form connections within the network. Members become concerned about sharing; some are fearful about security, the rise of malicious hacking and state surveillance having contributed to this. Inroads activists acknowledge that the feeling of anxiety creates isolation and impacts on the ability of members to connect with each other. The organisation thus focuses efforts on acknowledging the challenges, and examining and responding to them. Communication of solidarity is one valuable way of dealing with immediate challenges, particularly for those working with vulnerable groups and those working on edge of legality. A key response by inroads is to acknowledge that the challenges cannot be met alone. Collaboration provides ways to increase the power of the movement, and momentum builds further. Changes to cross-movement solidarities have occurred in response to the challenges, with a sense that there is less focus on defending the territories between organisations, less jockeying for position:

> There is greater sense of sharing the stage. Allies are becoming more visible; it feels hopeful. Where it goes is unknown. Particularly in the Global North, there is still a sense of being in a reactive mode. How those interested in working collaboratively and transparently move forward proactively – this is the question. (Interview with Katie Gillum, inroads co-convenor, 2018)

Focusing on research is key to the work of inroads. It enables the organisation to improve interventions that seek to challenge abortion stigma, to document abortion stigma and measure how it changes in different settings. The organisation achieves this in a number of ways: through academic publications, through supporting research, and by providing resources which can be used for lobbying purposes to inform policies on health systems, and evaluation programmes which can be shared within the network. Again, imbued within this aspect of the work is the importance of sharing and collaboration:

> It's about the democratisation of information; this is very important. The research is not just owned by one person or organisation; nor is much of what we do dependent on external timelines, such as long waiting times for academic publications. We can respond quickly via our network. We have seen collaborations between small NGOs and large NGOs emerge, working together on large-scale projects to tackle abortion stigma. (Interview with Katie Gillum, inroads co-convenor, 2018)

In terms of what lies ahead, inroads would like to see greater visibility of activists who are leading change in their communities. The organisation notes, for instance, the artist activists, and those working on migrant rights and anti-deportation – these are often the activists who are not seen or acknowledged as leading on challenging abortion stigma. Typically, these organisations are also working on intersecting stigmas, linked, for instance, to sexuality and sexual health. In the Global North these issues are often separated; because of religious beliefs, this is typically not the case in the Global South.

Inroads highlights the work of organisations such as Women's Global Network for Reproductive Rights (WGNRR), based in the Philippines, as a prime example of this. WGNRR is a grassroots organisation with reach throughout the Global South, which works to build and strengthen movements for sexual and reproductive health and rights (SRHR) and justice. Its work is targeted at those who are most marginalised, those who most lack economic, social and political power. WGNRR was also the first major organiser of the 'International Day for Access to Safe and Legal Abortion', which is held annually on 28 September. Its focus is to affirm the need for access to abortion and the need for abortion to be legal. Since 2011, WGNRR has spent extensive time and effort developing collaborative relationships around the globe, promoting the resulting campaign and providing a coordination role. In 2017, for instance, the organisation collaborated with inroads on a series of actions that centred global participation and local ownership on the theme #IResistWePersist. The coordination role is supported by the complementary efforts of other organisations, such as the International Campaign for Women's Right to Safe Abortion (whose work is detailed in the following case study) and inroads. The actions of the three organisations are complementary, with different audiences and purposes: the International Campaign, for instance, includes a focus on sustainable development goals; WGNNR focuses on the reproductive rights movement; and inroads focuses on gathering information about and highlighting work based on ending stigma, and supporting the community of practice that carries out this work.

In terms of future developments, inroads seeks to continue enabling connections to be made around the world, and to reach organisations that are working alone. Its vision is centred on a world without abortion stigma, where abortion is seen as common and necessary and not isolated from other reproductive health services such as family planning. Its wish list also includes having no limitations in the law, abortion imagery in the media being more reflective of reality, and funding of organisations being long-standing and not affected by issues such as the Global Gag Rule.

Networking and campaigning

The International Campaign for Women's Right to Safe Abortion (ICWRSA) was established in 2012. Its primary aim is to build an international network and campaign that brings together organisations with an interest in promoting and providing safe abortion to create a shared platform for advocacy, debate and dialogue, and the sharing of information, evidence, skills and experience. It positions safe abortion as both a public health issue and a human rights issue, and promotes the idea that women should have autonomy to make their own decisions about whether and when to have children, and access to the means of acting on those decisions without risk to their health or lives. The organisation also campaigns specifically for a moratorium on prosecutions for abortion and the removal of abortion from the criminal law (interview with Marge Berer, ICWRSA 2018). The organisation has a series of objectives centred around raising awareness of the impact of unsafe and illegal abortion, building strategic partnerships, and facilitating leadership among young women in the movement. Furthermore, it aims to share evidence-based information, standards and guidelines to inform and improve policy, programmes and practice, as well as developing and disseminating key messages to counter the influence of the anti-abortion movement and claim the language of abortion as a moral decision. It has a membership base of over 1,250 members in 117 countries. Its activities include the publication twice a week of a news report from around the world, a social media presence, and engagement with the press and media. It is also conducting research on court cases and imprisonment of women and providers for abortion, and is one of the coordinators of 'International Safe Abortion Day', which takes place on 28 September each year, to raise awareness and provide solidarity to those campaigning for safe abortion.

The global event provides a unique way in which organisations and individuals can organise actions and events to take place at the same time. It is also a means for them to express solidarity, and a vehicle for resistance to restricted access, as well as providing an opportunity to focus on unsafe abortion. Initially beginning in 1990 as a regional event in Latin America and the Caribbean, organised by the Campaña 28 de Septiembre (a regional network of activist groups), the event was later promoted by the Women's Global Network for Reproductive Rights as an international day, with activities spreading to other regions. In 2012, the year the International Campaign for Women's Right to Safe Abortion was initiated, the campaign also took a leading role in coordinating and promoting the event among partner organisations globally. Each year one or more themes serve to focus on grassroots and national activities to highlight the injustices of unsafe abortion. Typically groups in 45–60 countries organise and take part in events, which include an information campaign on abortion policy (Bangladesh), a feminist festival (Tokyo), a televised discussion programme on abortion stigma (Nigeria), a solidarity demonstration for Ireland (Northern India), a roundtable discussion on safe and legal abortion (Russia), an infographic on accessing legal abortion (Costa Rica), an advertising campaign on being Catholic and prochoice (US), a public march calling for abortion reform (the Republic of Ireland), a short film and workshop on how to talk about abortion (Northern Ireland) (International Campaign for Women's Right to Safe Abortion, 2015, 2016, 2017b).

The International Campaign for Women's Right to Safe Abortion also contributes to the evidence base, for example, by working with academics to publish research, contributing to social issue journals and in 2018 co-hosting and organising a small international conference. The campaign director coordinator, Marge Berer, notes that the aims of the organisation are broad and long-term and will take many years to implement. Achieving these aims is a significant challenge in a context of limited funding for advocates on the ground, especially those in middle-income countries who no longer qualify for much existing funding. In its first two years, the International Campaign for Women's Right to Safe Abortion itself relied on donations and contributions from a small number of international nongovernmental organisations and a few small, restricted grants; only in its third year has more substantial donor funding been offered.

Berer asserts that a significant development globally is the increased awareness of women's and girls' need for safe abortion in many countries, thanks both to increasing activism and access to medical abortion pills both within and outside of the law. As with other activist organisations, the prevalence of right-wing movements in some countries are challenging and reversing hard-won gains. "Campaign members say the existence of the campaign makes them feel they are not alone in this fight but are part of a movement that is sharing knowledge and experience and linking advocates together across the globe to promote and protect abortion rights" (interview with Marge Berer, ICWRSA, 2018).

Advocacy

As has been highlighted in Chapter Five, it has taken time for women's rights, and in particular abortion as a human right, to become a focus for mainstream human rights organisations. As the former head of Amnesty International's Gender Unit, Gita Sahgal, has stated with regard to women's and sexual rights: 'the formal human rights movement has been left behind by the activism and the transformative legal work that is taking place outside it' (Open Democracy, 2011). The development of international and regional human rights bodies' decisions and recommendations on access to abortion, and wider campaigning on violence against women and gender rights, has facilitated a move towards abortion being considered a legitimate mainstream human rights concern.

Mainstream campaigning and advocacy on abortion throws up challenges for larger human rights bodies. Human rights organisations are often supported by faith-based groups, some of whom oppose abortion. In such instances, the loss of support from highly influential groups such as churches (and their followers) must be taken into account when deciding to take a stance on abortion. In addition, personal perspectives and biases can make this issue more uncomfortable to discuss and may result in more barriers being put up against abortion campaigns (Pierson and Bloomer, 2017). However, it is vital that larger organisations take on women's rights, as legitimacy in the international sphere is hard to achieve without acknowledgement and recognition within a legal framework.

Amnesty International's 'My Body, My Rights' campaign is a useful example of mainstream human rights advocacy and campaigning on abortion. Amnesty International was set up in 1960 in response to the political imprisonment of students in Portugal. In the past 50 years it has expanded to become the largest and most well-known human rights organisation in the world. Its work primarily focuses on awareness raising, campaigning and lobbying, both in response to specific human rights abuses and through strategic campaigns on specific issues.

Up until 2007, Amnesty International had a neutral position on abortion. Following the launch of a campaign entitled 'Stop Violence Against Women', Amnesty defined its position on restricted abortion access in cases of rape as an act of violence against women:

> Amnesty International's position is not for abortion as a right but for women's human rights to be free of fear, threat and coercion as they manage all consequences of rape and other grave human rights violations. (Gilmore, in Amnesty International, 2007: 1)

It then noted that it was supportive of decriminalisation:

> to ensure women have access to health care when complications arise from abortion and to defend women's access to abortion, within reasonable gestational limits, when their health or human rights are in danger. (Amnesty International, 2007: 1)

From this initial limited position on abortion law and access, a campaign proposal was developed as part of the global focus on economic and social rights. This was accepted by members internally and later launched in 2014 as the My Body, My Rights campaign. The campaign, while global, was limited to one country per region area (these were Burkina Faso, El Salvador, the Republic of Ireland, Nepal and Morocco). Despite the focus on particular countries, the campaign also supported and promoted work in countries which had not been prioritised for the campaign, including Northern Ireland.

The My Body, My Rights campaign focused particularly on bodily autonomy and the theme of making decisions about, and having control of, one's body as a human right. This encompassed being able to make decisions about health, and sexual and reproductive lives 'being able to choose who to love, for instance, or if and when to marry and have children and to be able to make these decisions without fear, coercion, violence or discrimination' (Amnesty International, 2016: 1). As a global campaign, its message is broad in scope, with individual countries focusing on particular themes and building on the activism and advocacy work already taking place in each setting.

In Northern Ireland, Amnesty International took a decision to align the first stages of the campaign with the limited legal reforms proposed by the Minister of Justice. It commissioned public opinion polls which sought views on abortion provided on grounds of fatal foetal anomaly and sexual crime. It did not seek views on abortion more generally. In 2016 another opinion poll was commissioned which covered wider reform, including decriminalisation of abortion. Amnesty International later joined the judicial review action against the Department of Justice on legal reforms for fatal foetal anomaly and sexual crime, and in 2017, joined a case focusing on prosecution for procurement and usage of the abortion pill. However, as Pierson and Bloomer (2017) argue in their analysis of human rights discourses and abortion in Northern Ireland, the initial focus on cases related to fatal foetal anomaly and sexual crime meant that the decriminalisation message became lost within the first stages of the campaign.

The short duration of the Amnesty International global My Body, My Rights campaign means that it is too early to assess the impact of tangible changes. However, what the campaign does illustrate is the momentum and interest which a large organisation can bring to abortion rights and the widespread and systematic nature of reproductive rights violations globally.

Conclusions

This chapter has presented a sample of the variety of abortion activism which is occurring globally at this moment in time. The shape and organisation of such a variety of groups illustrates the scope of different actions and resistances needed to counter restrictive abortion access worldwide. The chapter provides a snapshot of how those advocating for abortion access adopt a range of strategies which may provide practical short-term help or envision a longer-term change in legal and policy regimes or a complete overhaul of societal perceptions of women and their bodily autonomy. Linking and underscoring the wide range of activism presented in this chapter is the belief that this is necessary and important work that will contribute to the achievement of full rights and citizenship for women within society.

SEVEN

Is choice enough? Engaging with reproductive justice

Introduction

The preceding chapters have presented the legal, political and discursive frameworks surrounding abortion access and activism. In this chapter, we consider to what extent the framework of choice may be superseded by reproductive justice. Reproductive justice is a concept that emerged within the US, from a group of African American women. It is interlinked with frameworks of reproductive health and rights, and is defined by three key principles:

> The right to have a child; the right not to have a child; the right to parent children in safe and healthy environments. (Ross and Solinger, 2017: 9)

The core recognition of the right to have children and families, along with the right not to, is critical, as is centring the needs of people and communities who have been marginalised and disempowered by systems of oppression. The Reproductive Justice Framework recognises that particular groups of women, such as indigenous women, women of colour and women in low-income groups are disproportionately affected by attempts to control their reproductive lives.[*] Advocates have repeatedly demonstrated, through a focus on lived experiences of women and the wider community, that racism affects the reproductive rights and health of women of colour, as too does economic status, thus affecting their reproductive freedom. Core to the framework is the argument that achieving reproductive justice entails access to material resources which enable:

> high quality health care, housing and education, a living wage, a healthy environment and a safety net for when

---

[*] We use the phrase 'women of colour' to reflect the terminology used by the reproductive justice movement.

these resources fail. Safe and dignified fertility management, childbirth and parenting are impossible without these resources. (Ross and Solinger, 2017: 9)

The Reproductive Justice Framework is informed by a historical analysis of reproductive injustices, alongside analysis of legal, policy and technological contexts. The reproductive injustices in the US have a long history, from rape and forced pregnancy in the slavery era to the population control of Native American communities.

The history of reproductive injustice against the black community has been charted by Dorothy Roberts, Harvard Law professor, whose interest was sparked by the focus on 'crack babies' in the latter part of the twentieth century, and the particular attack on black mothers in this campaign. Roberts (2017) begins by telling the story of reproductive oppressions experienced by the black community with a focus on the slavery era, documenting repeated incidents of sexual assaults, mistreatment of women while pregnant, deliberate breaking-up of families and forced marriage. The legal prohibition of slavery in the US in 1865 resulted in greater freedom for the black community, but systemic racism has remained a dominant feature of American society, and is exhibited by old and new forms of reproductive oppression. In the twentieth century, government policy under the banner of population control operated to the detriment of women of colour and those in low-income groups. This included, for instance, welfare caps on those with large families, with the stereotype inaccurately portraying women of colour and those in low-income groups as overrepresented. In the 1930s mass sterilisations occurred, many under state law, with upwards of 20,000 women affected, most of whom were African American and Native American women. Sterilisation was used as a tool to achieve 'better breeding', a policy imbued with values of eugenics and white supremacy (Silliman et al, 2016: 59; Amy and Rowlands, 2018). Coerced or forced sterilisation continued throughout the twentieth century and into the early part of the twenty-first century, with recent reported instances of women in prisons in California being sterilised without full consent as late as 2010 (California State Auditor, 2014).

Women of colour have also been targets of unwarranted control of fertility with hormones. This includes unethical testing of birth control medication, aggressive marketing of long-acting contraceptives and inadequate testing of abortion medication (Roberts, 2017). In the 1990s racism also led to criminalisation of those who presented with drug addictions while pregnant, with women of colour, especially black women, overrepresented among those prosecuted, even though their rates of illegal drug use were not proportionately higher. In such instances, adequate health support for the drug addiction was not available; few facilities could take new clients and fewer still would allow children to be resident with their mothers. In other examples, women of colour presented at court were offered long-acting contraception in lieu of a shorter jail sentence (Roberts, 2017: 151). At the time of such cases, long-acting contraceptives such as Norplant were offered to black communities through incentive programmes, with little consideration of side effects. Some discovered that having been able to have Norplant inserted as part of Medicaid, a government-funded programme, they had to pay for the removal themselves. For those on low incomes this was often unachievable, and long waiting lists for removal also posed problems (Roberts, 2017: 130). Such practices served to alienate women of colour from family planning services and led to decades of distrust of public health (Silliman et al, 2016).

The Native American communities in the US (and Canada) were subject to particular policies that sought to undermine their culture, land sovereignty and family structures. Beginning in the nineteenth century, children were removed from families and placed in boarding schools where cultural assimilation to Western, Christian values was the norm. These institutions were later identified as sites for widespread physical, emotional and sexual abuse (Smith, 2015). Many other children were fostered or adopted by families outside of Native American communities at rates much higher than other communities. Such practices continued in the twentieth century and early part of the twenty-first century (Smith, 2015; Silliman et al, 2016: 112). In her detailed examination of the sexual violence experienced by Native Americans and genocide of their communities, Smith (2015: 10) explains how colonial positioning of the indigenous population as both 'dirty' and polluted with sexual sin also included a view that they were sexually violable, 'rapeable', and ultimately not entitled to bodily integrity. Coerced and forced sterilisation trends and overemphasis of long-acting contraceptives among Native American women mirror the experiences of the black community.

The communities from islands of the Asia-Pacific region have also experienced specific challenges to their reproductive rights, including issues related to language barriers and immigration. These are linked to stereotypes that Asian-Pacific women are either hypersexualised or sexually repressed. These communities have also suffered from stereotypes of excessive fertility, cultural inferiority and pressure to culturally assimilate (Silliman et al, 2016: 221). These assumptions typically ignore the cultural, linguistic and religious diversity within each community. In addition, women and girls are trafficked illegally from countries across Asia and forced to work in the US in settings of domestic work, sweatshops and the sex trade. As a result of this trafficking, the women and girls are extremely vulnerable to physical, sexual and emotional violence. Unwanted pregnancies, forced abortions and sexually transmitted infections are common, alongside no access to medical care (Nakae, 2017: 1).

The reproductive oppression experienced by women of colour in the US mobilised organisations on behalf of themselves and their communities. The Reproductive Justice Framework recognises that women of colour have been at the forefront of highlighting injustices and campaigning for change. During the twentieth century a number of activist groups took the lead in fighting for reproductive rights. The National Black Feminist Organization, for instance, played a crucial role in reframing birth control and abortion, linking reproductive rights to the civil rights struggle (Silliman et al, 2016: 62). The Combahee River Collective, a black feminist lesbian organisation active in Boston, critiqued racism, sexism, poverty and heterosexism from a strong ideological standpoint, as well as celebrating links to the history of black protest. Black women such as Faye Wattleton led the fight for justice from within mainstream organisations such as Planned Parenthood, while others within the health sector, such as Joycelyn Elders, Surgeon General, rose to prominent roles within the US government.

Within the Native American community, organisations such as Women of All Red Nations, the Mother's Milk Project and the Native American Women's Health Education Resource Center worked to counteract the cultural destruction of their communities, focusing on issues such as establishing native schools, taking control of boarding schools where children had been sent to live away from their communities, highlighting environmental injustices, and improving access to abortion and other health services.

The efforts of a wide range of organisations were brought together by the SisterSong collective in 1997. Women of colour organisations came together to use their collective power to build a grassroots movement (Silliman et al, 2016: 49). Initially focused on gaps in reproductive health services with the aim of tacking issues such as reproductive health infections, the SisterSong organisation began collecting and sharing data on reproductive health, experiences of treatment and prevention STIs, and highlighting societal factors that impact the reproductive health of women of colour (Ross et al, 2001). Since its inception, SisterSong has provided a platform to highlight the continuing reproductive oppressions experienced by women of colour and to foster collective action on addressing injustices. Its members have raised awareness of the health needs of their communities, focusing on education, research and lobbying. The Reproductive Justice Framework situates itself as intersectional in nature, influenced by the seminal work of Kimberlé Crenshaw (1991):

> based on the understanding that the impacts of race, class, gender and sexual identity oppressions are not additive but integrative, producing this paradigm of intersectionality. For each individual and each community, the effects will be different, but they share some of the basic characteristics of intersectionality – universality, simultaneity and interdependence. (Ross, 2011: 1)

The notion of 'choice' as the overarching framework is rejected in light of the multiple and interconnected constraints faced by those affected. For example, 'A woman who decided to have an abortion out of economic necessity does not experience "choice"' (Silliman et al, 2016: 12). Nor do those who have limited access to contraceptives experience choice, or those who do not have access to national health services or health insurance due to their ethnicity, immigration or economic status. The foundations of the Reproductive Justice Framework are informed by principles of social justice and human rights. Its proponents firmly reject the 'choice' framework for a series of reasons:

- Choice does not speak to the complexities of women's lives. It excludes the lack of access women face and the depth of women's experiences. No woman seeking an abortion ever has just one human rights issue confronting her.
- Choice leaves out opposition to population control. Reproductive choice in the US only speaks to the right not to have a child, but it does not address a woman's right to have as many children as she wants.
- Choice is a politically conservative concept. In order to fight conservative politics in the 1970s, the movement made 'choice' a libertarian antigovernment concept that would appeal to larger segments of the population, which de-emphasised women's rights, sex rights and sexual pleasure, and failed to support women as moral decision makers.
- Choice is a consumerist or marketplace concept. Abortion is a reproductive right that is only available to those who can afford it.

The marketplace privatises the governmental obligation not only to protect choice but to ensure that choices are achievable for all.

- Choice is an individual concept that does not address the social problems that prohibit women from exercising their rights. Unplanned pregnancies and poverty are not an individual woman's problems.
- Choice primarily resonates with those who feel they can make choices in other areas of their lives, those whose human rights are less likely to be violated.
- Choice is not a sufficiently powerful moral argument, especially when you have to challenge the 'life' framework of those opposed to women's rights.
- Choice is not a compelling vision. It's not the vision needed to mobilise the kind of movement capable of winning clear and consistent victories. (Gerber-Fried, cited in Ross, 2011).

Ross and Solinger (2017: 124–5) also identify the arguments of activist Tannia Espara in critiquing the choice framework, that individual rights are superseded by 'whole people, whole families, whole communities'. The components of individual rights to:

> Choice, privacy, freedom from interference and personal autonomy are all necessary for all women to achieve reproductive rights, but they are also completely insufficient … [they] do not actually guarantee women's access to those rights in a society. Where sexism, racism, economic exploitation and bias against immigrants flourish. Invoking individual rights or even constitutional protections of those rights does not accomplish what could, in fact, be accomplished through altered power relations, including the shifting of resources to people who currently lack them. (Ross and Solinger, 2017: 124)

It is this framing which sets reproductive justice apart from choice. In the US this rejection of the choice framework placed reproductive justice advocates, for a time, in a contrasting position to many mainstream organisations who focused solely on improving access to abortion. The context here is important: the role of women of colour as activists and their approach to reproductive justice has often received much less attention within society, in contrast to the work of mainstream organisations led by the white middle and upper classes. Particularly in the latter part of the twentieth century, these mainstream organisations were criticised for not appropriately recognising the needs of women of colour and low-income groups, and the role played by reproductive justice organisations in the injustices faced by these groups (Silliman et al, 2016). An example of this is the pushback from mainstream groups who did not want further regulation of sterilisation – this came against a backdrop of white women who wanted easier access to sterilisation, with some groups opposing additional regulation. These groups failed to see how regulation was needed to minimise poor practice that had resulted in many women of colour being sterilised without full consent (Silliman et al, 2016). In the early part of the twenty-first century it was evident, however, that the disconnection between mainstream organisations and women of colour communities was easing. A greater diversity of leadership became evident, with strategic alliances emerging from collaboration between organisations. Networks developed further, drawing in new organisations and communities. Reflecting on the changes, Marlene Gerber Fried observed:

> Most important, Reproductive Justice, a trend led by women of colour and their allies and younger women, has breathed new life into the movement and is becoming the dominant framework. Placing reproductive rights in the struggle for social justice and human rights has global resonance and it is a compelling, expansive, and inclusive vision for US activists. (Gerber Fried, 2013: 13)

It is of note that within the US a minority is resistant to accepting the Reproductive Justice Framework. Jon O'Brien from Catholics for Choice has argued that the choice framework could not be simply replaced by reproductive justice and that focusing on too broad a framework lessens the focus on abortion rights (O'Brien, 2013). Gerber Fried et al (2013) argue that the shift from choice to reproductive justice does not devalue the autonomy of women; instead, it positions it within human rights framing. It has not negated the choice argument but integrated and reframed it within reproductive justice. The tension within this debate indicates that for some there is a preference for different frameworks, one narrow and the other much broader, and also perhaps a misunderstanding of the fundamentals of reproductive justice: abortion rights are core to establishing full reproductive autonomy for all women and ending all reproductive injustices. Other commentators external to the movement have been more supportive of the Reproductive Justice Framework, providing commentary on challenges as a reminder to be wary of a complete reliance on, for instance, human rights framing of reproductive oppressions. These commentators have noted that often human rights are positioned as interchangeable with social justice, and that advocates need to be cognisant of the weaknesses within the human rights approach. For example, Rebouche (2016) notes that within a human rights framework, abortion rights arguments have typically focused on access to abortion under specific conditions, such as when a woman's life or health is at risk, or in cases of sexual crime. Although recent recommendations from human rights bodies have highlighted the need for decriminalisation, such bodies have shied away from advocating for abortion on request.

Enforcing human rights is problematic, as discussed in Chapter Five, and while the human rights approach has served to highlight specific countries with restrictive abortion laws, the influence of a Global North imbued with conservatism and imperialism poses problems. Historically, it has failed to provide a comprehensive analysis of race and socioeconomic issues (Lewis, 2003; Rebouche, 2016). However, while the challenges of the human rights approach have been recognised by reproductive justice advocates, human rights lawyers and human rights organisations remain largely focused on abortion rights (Rebouche, 2016: 22). Such weaknesses have been counteracted with a critical race approach within the Reproductive Justice Framework, and criticism of the choice framework. Using a holistic, grassroots, community-based, participatory approach has ensured that reproductive justice organisations do not rely on courts to achieve outcomes. The Reproductive Justice Framework has provided a vehicle by which to address a raft of reproductive oppressions in the US, though, as noted, challenges remain. What we seek to explore in the sections that follow is how the same principles apply elsewhere in the world. As demonstrated in the following discussions, while terminology may vary, the Reproductive Justice Framework has been applied to different contexts around the world, a trend also observed by Silliman et al (2016), who commented that in the US many communities were applying the framework before the terminology existed.

Before proceeding, it is worth noting the position of Marge Berer from the International Campaign for Women's Right to Safe Abortion, who cautions not to focus too heavily on terminology. Berer notes that adoption of new terminology tends to be slow, hampered by language barriers, and that changes in terminology can be problematic for some of those working in restricted contexts:

'I'll never forget a conference I went to many years ago where someone stood up and said: "They used to call it family planning. Now they call it reproductive health ... They used to call it ...", and a bit later made the remark that his country still didn't have any of it and that the change of terminology was making it all very difficult, not least because it meant policy and documents etc. all had to be changed.' (Interview with Berer, 2018)

Indeed, in many settings, the use of particular words remains a taboo. In Eastern Europe, for instance in Romania, the word 'abortion' is rarely used.

In the section that follows we will consider how the *content* of reproductive justice is applied, and linked with it, how terminology is also impacted.

Global perspectives on reproductive justice

Anthropologist Lynn M. Morgan presents an insightful perspective on terminology in an exploration of reproductive justice and reproductive rights in Argentina. Morgan (2015) tells the story of how, upon speaking at a conference of feminist anthropologists in Argentina, she was taken aback at their reluctance to take up her suggestion that they shift the focus from reproductive rights to reproductive justice. She had framed this debate on the basis that the anti-abortion movement had hijacked rights–based arguments to reposition the debate from one about access to abortion to one of foetal rights and parental rights. She argued that if a rights-based approach was being adopted by conservative forces, then perhaps the concept of rights had outlived its usefulness (Morgan, 2016: 137). What Morgan had failed to comprehend was that the framing of access to abortion as a human rights issue carried significant symbolism in Argentina, being linked to a history of political struggle and the aftermath of political dictatorship. Human rights discourse and processes such as truth commissions had formed a key part of the country's recovery from widespread human rights abuses. Human rights formed a key platform of two successive presidencies. This was exemplified by the country being the first in Latin America to legalise same-sex marriage in 2010, and in 2012 it passed the world's most progressive gender identity law. While it introduced a comprehensive sexual health programme, abortion remained problematic. Abortion is permitted on grounds of risk to the woman's life or health, or if the pregnancy is the result of sexual assault. In practice, however, abortion on legal grounds is often denied. Illegal abortion is common, with complications from unsafe abortion being the leading cause of maternal mortality in the last two decades (Ramos et al, 2014).

Despite the problems arising from unsafe abortion, attempts at legal reform were thwarted up until 2018. Then, when building on a campaign against femicides called Ni Una Menos (Not One Less), the efforts of campaigners resulted in a bill progressing in parliament that would allow abortion up to 14 weeks of pregnancy (Politi, 2018). The bill failed to gain sufficient support in the senate, but served as a signifier of widespread public support for reform. Previous to this, the progress made on issues such as gender identity, buoyed by a human rights approach, remained in stark contrast to the lack of progress on abortion. The reasons for this are complex, and linked to issues such as a strong maternal culture, abortion stigma and the high-profile anti-abortion position of the Catholic Church. Intertwined with this is the legacy of the dictatorship, and the position of the Madres in Argentine society, a group of women who fought tirelessly to raise the issue of the thousands who had disappeared during state terror campaigns. The symbolism of the Madres, highlighting the human rights abuses committed upon their offspring, has been used by both anti-abortion and prochoice lobby groups. Despite the hurdles, the feminist campaigners that Morgan spoke to remained determined to continue campaigning using human rights as a framing. They were reluctant, for instance, to frame access to abortion as a health issue, fearing that this would result in medicalisation and overregulation. Instead, the human rights framing allowed them to build on achievements brought about using human rights, to use internal human rights treaties, to apply pressure to politicians and to build on the solid foundation of scholarly work within Argentina on sexual and reproductive rights, which draws on a range of social justice movements including those focused on poverty, agrarian reform and indigenous identity politics (Morgan, 2015: 144). Morgan concludes her consideration of the reproductive justice versus reproductive rights framing by noting that while different dynamics are at play between the US and Argentina in the application of reproductive justice, both are in fact focused on a series of intersecting issues, recognising that abortion cannot be treated as a single-issue battle. Cognisant of history and context, human rights terminology carries more weight in Argentina; it is more palatable to the government than it is in the US.

One issue with the justice versus rights debate discussed in much of the literature cited is that 'rights' is seen as a static concept. However, the history of human rights advocacy, especially in the Global South, is that this concept has been contested. Social movements have played a significant role in seeking to transform these understandings of the concept of 'rights'. For example, the first significant covenant that emerged in the immediate aftermath of the Second World War centred on civil and political rights, with an emphasis on the rights of the individual as conceived by liberal philosophy. In later years, through the efforts of activists, this approach broadened to bring about a focus on the collective, through covenants on economic, social and cultural rights. The concept of reproductive rights with international covenants has been contested, however, as discussed in Chapter Five. This was exemplified by the position of theocratic states who continued to assert that no new rights were established at the International Conference on Population and Development (ICPD) in Cairo in 1994. Indeed, the lobbying of conservative faith-based organisations and theocratic states resulted in a more conservative content of the Cairo Declaration than had been anticipated, as discussed in Chapter Four. Another example is the way that human rights are viewed as a contentious framing. In Northern Ireland, for example, in the aftermath of the conflict, human rights have been positioned as a concern for the Catholic/ Nationalist/Republican community and not the Protestant/Unionist/ Loyalist community (Pierson and Bloomer, 2017). All of this points to the importance of context, which in turn circumscribes meanings, terminology and political possibilities.

Exploring the less controversial concept of reproductive health extends this argument. In cases where there is an extremely difficult cultural climate for women's rights in general, much less for reproductive rights, activists have used the concept of reproductive health and maternal mortality to push forward some progress on abortion. This is exemplified in the Philippines where there is provision for humane post-abortion care, which is used as a wedge, both in discussions and in actual delivery, to work for abortion access. When abortion is illegal and maternal mortality from unsafe abortion is high, it is clear that abortion can be easily positioned as a public health issue. This raises the question of whether health aspects become more obscured the further a state moves away from criminalisation. This is an issue which has not largely been explored in the literature. And does this mean that the closer a state is to decriminalisation, the more easily human rights arguments can be made? We reflect on this further in the concluding chapter.

Those countries where access to abortion is severely restricted are often those for whom applying the lens of reproductive justice highlights the multiple, complex issues experienced by women and girls. In these countries a holistic approach to considering the positioning of sexual and reproductive health reveals significant disparities. In Egypt, for instance, high levels of poverty, which have increased significantly in the last decade, also reveal that women are three times more likely to experience poverty than men. Food insecurity is prevalent, resulting in malnutrition and related health problems (Government of the Arab Republic of Egypt and United National Population Fund, 2013). This has an impact on the ability of those affected to participate fully in society, to access education and employment, for instance. Access to sexual and reproductive health services is constrained by economic barriers and delivery of services aimed at those who are married. Sex outside marriage is regarded in many communities as a taboo, and those identified as having committed this transgression are liable to be ostracised. Female genital mutilation is common, and despite a ban introduced in 2008, it is estimated that 90% of women and girls have been subjected to the practice. Marriage below the legal age has been identified as a particular problem, with evidence suggesting that many girls are subjected to 'marriage tourism', whereby they are removed from the country in order to marry older men (RESURJ et al, 2015b). A law introduced in 2016, which applies if the girl/woman is 25 years younger than her prospective husband, requires the man to deposit money (circa £4,500) into a bank account in the woman's name prior to the marriage taking place. The legislation has been widely criticised, however, as it effectively permits human trafficking. The law is a revised version of an earlier law which banned such marriages. The original law was reviewed and the financial penalty added following pressure from Islamic groups (Farid, 2016).

In Egypt, the societal norms of marrying young, expectations of having children and inadequate access to family planning mean that the adolescent pregnancy rate is high. The maternal mortality rate is also high, particularly among the poor and those in rural areas, with a fragmented health infrastructure unable to effectively meet the needs of the population. Access to abortion is severely restricted, with legal abortions largely available only if the woman's life is at risk. Data on unsafe abortion is scarce. In addition to this, intimate partner violence is common, and gender inequalities are evident across a range of indicators. In sum, to be a woman or girl in Egypt means experiencing a range of socioeconomic, cultural and health injustices. Sustained widespread reforms are the solutions to such injustices.

One country which has centred reproductive justice within government policy is South Africa. In 2014, Bathabile Dlamini, the country's Minister of Social Development, announced that the position of the ruling party, the ANC, and that of the government, was firmly grounded in reproductive justice. In discussing abortion, she noted:

> We realise that it [abortion] is but one of the reproductive experiences of women that needs to be enabled. We are also concerned about improving other elements of women's reproductive experiences, such as improving women's economic and educational statuses, we are concerned about whether women are in violent or abusive situations, whether their children have access to nutritious food, housing, clothing and other social protection services. (Dlamini, 2014)

This was a landmark moment in the history of the reproductive justice movement, signalling that the framework's use as a foundation for government policy was possible. The extent to which this has been possible remains subject to scrutiny. The framework itself has been subject to further exploration in the South African and British context, with a proposition that it could be applied in conjunction with a reparative justice approach to meet the needs of particular contexts (Macleod et al, 2016; Macleod, 2018).

The reparative justice approach begins with the recognition when injustice has occurred, when harm has been experienced and that the person/community should be able to access recompense as a result. Drawing on the work of Ernesto Verdeja's (2008) critical theory of reparative justice, Macleod et al (2016) propose that abortion should be considered from four conceptual perspectives:

- Individual material dimension – the facilitation of autonomous decision-making with regard to the outcome of a pregnancy. Key requirements: Legislative enablement and supportive healthcare provision.
- Individual symbolic dimension – the understanding of individual lived experiences of unsupportable pregnancies. Key requirements: The understanding of abortion within the social and structural dynamics of local settings.
- Collective material dimension – the provision of legal state-sponsored healthcare resources which make abortion accessible and safe for all women. Key requirements: Well-funded, widely available, legal healthcare resources.

- Collective symbolic dimension – the ways in which public discourses about and social attitudes to abortion construct available subject positions for women seeking abortions.

These conceptual lenses are applied to an analysis of a country's abortion laws, access and discourses indicating individual and collective reparations. For instance, from an individual material dimension, this leads to the conceptualisation of 'the facilitation of autonomous decision-making regarding the outcome of a pregnancy via legislative enablement and a commitment to supportive healthcare provision' (Macleod et al, 2016: 604). From a collective material dimension, the conceptualisation is 'the redistribution of economic resources so as to ensure that those affected are able to access the resources they need' (Macleod et al, 2016: 604). Applying the reparative framework to abortion, the authors state that two forms of reparation are required:

- transformation of the social conditions that generate unwanted pregnancies and render them unsupportable;
- the provision of social and material support for women to end pregnancies that they do not want or decide that they are unable to continue with (Macleod et al, 2016: 610).

In applying the reparative justice framework to South Africa, the authors note that two areas of priority emerge: first, in relation to health infrastructure, it is evident that significant improvements are needed to ensure adequate provision of safe abortion services; second, the societal positioning of abortion needs to be addressed to remove stigmatisation. In the second case study area, Britain, the authors note that while abortion is readily available to the majority of abortion seekers, the means by which it is currently accessed, through a medical approach, with two doctors required to sign off the procedure, which is restricted to clinic or hospital settings, fails to recognise women's bodily autonomy and fails to provide equality of access. The application of a reparative justice analysis centres women within legislation, allows for abortion to be accessed away from clinical settings and redresses how those seeking abortion are depicted in society. Women should thus be positioned as central to reform and provided with space to share their stories (Macleod et al, 2016: 612).

Applying a reproductive justice approach to the British context illustrates how the Global North perspective can potentially 'divorce women's rights from projects that target international economic relations, or the inequalities produced by the global economy'

(Rebouche, 2016: 21). The choice approach has been the dominant influence in abortion rights campaigns in Britain, influenced by second wave feminist activism. However, the choice approach fails to interrogate how much free choice is actually involved in reproductive health decisions. The austerity policies that have been in place since 2008 (since the financial crisis of 2007/08) have direct and indirect effects on women's reproductive 'choices'. For example, the 'rape clause' proposed by the Conservative government in 2017 within a child tax credit reform measure (child tax credits are means-tested support for anyone who supports a child as a parent or with parental responsibilities) restricts access to claiming for two children. A third child can only be claimed for if the pregnancy resulted from a sexual crime or the child was conceived during an abusive relationship. The policy requires a woman to state the circumstances for this to claim for the third child. The impact of such a policy, as well as being a potential human rights violation, indicates that for women with less socioeconomically secure circumstances, there is little to gain from a simple choice perspective on abortion rights, as choice is mediated through potential poverty. The Reproductive Justice Framework gives a much fuller understanding of choices in contemporary Britain in the context of austerity, withdrawal from the European Union and the resulting impact on immigration status, and increased numbers of displaced people seeking refuge from crisis situations. As such, choice analysis is useful on its own only for a very small and specific group of women.

Case Study: RESURJ

Realizing Sexual and Reproductive Justice (RESURJ) is a transnational, Global South-led, membership-based alliance of feminist activists under the age of 40. It is grounded in national and regional social justice movements working across generations, constituencies and identities, seeking to realise sexual and reproductive justice for all. The alliance asserts that key to its efforts is the meaningful participation of younger feminists in shaping and advocating for transparent, accountable and sustainable development policies and programmes (interview with Marisa Viana, RESURJ, 2018).

RESURJ centres a justice approach that "encompasses an understanding of and a commitment to addressing the interlinkages between our bodies, our health and our human rights in the context of the ecological, economic and social crises" (interview with Marisa Viana, RESURJ, 2018). This approach also recognises historic injustices and systemic inequalities in gender power relations. The organisation aims to contribute to creating long-term systemic change by transforming ways of thinking, working and living, while relying on the leadership of communities most impacted by sexual and reproductive oppression. This recognition of the need to work within communities most affected mirrors that of many of the activist organisations featured in the previous chapter on activism and is core to the organisation's long-term goal: to work as a feminist global collective grounded in national realities to advocate for funding, policies and programmes that ensure equitable access to sexual and reproductive health services and information, including for safe abortion; protection of sexual rights and reproductive rights; the achievement of gender equality; comprehensive sexuality education; non-discrimination; and meaningful participation of young feminists in women's and feminist movements across Africa, Asia-Pacific, Latin America and the Middle East.

Since RESURJ was created in 2010, its core aim to position the voices of feminists from the Global South advocating for sexual, reproductive and gender justice in intergovernmental spaces has remained the same. Over time, however, RESURJ has refined its approach, in recognition of a deeper understanding of the interlinkage between sexual and reproductive justice, and economic, ecological and environmental justice, as a political strategy to advance women's and girl's rights and wellbeing. More recently, it has shifted focus from influencing the development of global-level intergovernmental processes such as the ICPD review and the 2030 Agenda for Sustainable Development, to further support movement-building and organising with young feminist activists at the regional and national levels for accountability for these agreements: "For us, going full circle meant that now we must see the policies we advocated for at the global level, actually become concrete changes in women and girls lives where it matters most, at the local level" (interview with Marisa Viana, RESURJ, 2018).

Achieving these aims, however, presents four key challenges. First is the lack of political will on the part of governments to uphold rights and adopt comprehensive policies to bring about justice:

'Despite numerous international and regional agreements, and national pledges and commitments, women and girls, in particular adolescent girls, LBTQI, black, indigenous, migrant, poor and women living with disabilities, among others pushed into marginalisation, continue to face stigma and discrimination, violence, sexual and reproductive rights violations and threats to their livelihoods.' (Interview with Marisa Viana, RESURJ, 2018)

Injustices related to bodily autonomy, mobility, freedom, and sexual and reproductive rights are further exacerbated by a range of crises: ecological degradation, militarisation and conflict, unjust financial trade governance, wealth concentration, and land and resource grabbing. RESURJ argues that the commitments made by countries to uphold gender equality and sexual and reproductive health rights lack substance and financial resources. A lack of political will, restrictive laws and policies, as well as the overreliance on penal policies that do not address the complex needs of women, all combine to make progress deeply problematic.

The second main barrier identified by RESURJ is the rise of conservatism, which as noted in the previous chapter, has been accompanied by a backlash, both globally and nationally, against gains made for the protection of sexual and reproductive rights and gender equality:

> 'From economic austerity measures and growing intolerance toward gender diversity, including conservative attacks on education policy in Brazil, the deepening inequalities through increased neoliberal policy in Mexico, to the rise of religious conservatism threatening abortion rights in the UK, to the worst crackdowns on sexual diversity in Egypt in two decades. This alarming trend has made our advocacy work more difficult, but extremely pertinent and urgent.' (Interview with Marisa Viana, RESURJ, 2018)

RESURJ identifies the third challenge to its work as the shifting focus away from the Commission on the Status of Women and the Commission on Population and Development in the global development agenda, the 2030 Agenda. Both of these intergovernmental spaces were widely recognised as providing key opportunities where women's and girls' rights have been elevated over the last 23 years. However, the adoption in 2015 of the new global development agenda, Agenda 2030, has led to diminishing the importance of the Commission on the Status of Women and the Commission on Population and Development, leading to a shift towards conservative discourse on population and development, and the loss of previously held gains in sexual and reproductive health and rights language. While attempts have been made to address the importance of linking these intergovernmental spaces and uphold the spirit of the conference of the 1990s, which recognised women's rights as human rights, these have not been wholly successful, and the concern is that institutional knowledge is being lost, resulting in gaps in access for those who relied on the intergovernmental spaces to elevate their priorities.

Finally, again mirroring the challenge of many other activist organisations, is the question of how the organisation itself can respond to the changing global and national landscape, while meeting the needs of members:

> 'Some members have been struggling to consistently contribute on a voluntary basis to an alliance that is leading significant advocacy and thought leadership work without prioritising paid work. This has led us to start a series of discussions around how we can better support our members, strengthen our networks and alliances, practise collective care as a movement strategy, and constantly check ourselves to ensure that we practise the feminist accountability with each other and the movement.' (Interview with Marisa Viana, RESURJ, 2018)

While the adoption of the Sustainable Development Goals presents its own set of challenges, RESURJ also views it as an opportunity to advance sexual, reproductive and gender justice from an intersectional approach. The 2030 Agenda for Sustainable Development presents opportunities to demand accountability for the challenges identified, at national, regional and global levels. With this new agenda, there is greater possibility for younger feminists to continue to organise around a shared agenda to break silos and strengthen activism for human rights, economic justice, bodily autonomy and the sustainability of the planet. This is also an opportunity for advancing new thinking about accountability, including developing alternative data collection indicators for development that take into account peoples lived realities and new language for advocacy. Continued advocacy around the High-level Political Forum at the UN (the body entrusted with follow-up and review of the 2030 Agenda), rooted in national experiences and regional movement-building, provides activists with the opportunity to hold governments accountable for realising justice for women and girls at the global level.

RESURJ asserts that the linkages between gender justice, and environmental and economic justices are all critical to building sustained movements and actions. Organising dialogues and actions cross-regionally, which strengthens cross-movement and cross-regional sharing, enhances the links between economic, environmental, and sexual and reproductive justice. While there is deeper awareness of the need to strengthen the connections across the various dimensions of sustainable development, the organisation recognises that in order for concrete gains to be made, it must continue to work to make these connections visible; and central to the implementation of the 2030 Agenda, it notes that while governments and diverse stakeholders have all adopted the interlinkage discourse, this is often without the real analysis and attention needed.

RESURJ's vision for the future is that it will continue to be a platform "where younger feminist advocates can come together to strategise, amplify our political voices, practise solidarity and challenge structural inequalities" (interview with Marisa Viana, RESURJ, 2018). In particular, it seeks to solidify its strong role as a facilitator at regional levels, to continue to be a leader in positioning an intersectional approach to sustainable development and sexual and reproductive justice, so that it can continue to make concrete proposals to challenge the reductionist approach to sexuality and reproduction. Finally, it aims to "have a new generation of members from the Global South continue to lead RESURJ with a strong feminist political voice, care for each other and the movement, and commitment to a culture of activism that integrates pleasure and joy" (interview with Marisa Viana, RESURJ, 2018).

An inherent value in the RESURJ approach to sexual and reproductive justice is 'nothing about us without us'. Those affected by law, policy and practice must be at the heart of the process, from the outset. Their voices, alongside comprehensive evidence that understands the structural inequalities and the complexities of people's lives, should inform debates about new legislation, policy and practice, and reviews to enable identification of the impact and effectiveness of such measures in peoples' lives.

Conclusion

As this chapter has illustrated, abortion cannot be viewed as a single issue, without consideration of the positioning of women in society. It cannot be separated from issues of race, ethnicity, sexuality, immigration, class or environment. The Reproductive Justice Framework allows for an analysis of historical and contemporary matters, and the identification of oppressions, and most importantly, has centred the voices of those directly impacted by oppression at its core. The collective approach of those affected at the heart of the movement has ensured a core value of 'nothing about us, without us'.

The analysis in this chapter has identified how the terminology used is often dependent on context. In some contexts reproductive justice values are evident, even if the framework is not formally invoked. This chapter has also identified global trends in reproductive justice, including how the framework has been hailed by the South African government as a foundation of its policies. This contrasts significantly with, for instance, US policy, both at home and abroad.

Reflecting on the analysis throughout this chapter, it is evident that the reproductive justice perspective is presenting new and exciting analytical tools with which to investigate women's reproductive life and choices globally and has thus the potential to make a significant contribution to academic understanding and policy reform.

EIGHT

Conclusion

The politicisation of abortion and its study by academics is a relatively new phenomenon. Arguably driven by legislative changes in the US and in Britain in the 1960s and '70s, feminist and gendered analysis of abortion and factors surrounding its enablement and restriction is becoming prolific and constitutes a field of study in itself. As we note particularly in Chapter Seven on reproductive justice, the study of abortion is bound into wider reproductive healthcare rights and restrictions, and also from a feminist intersectional perspective, identities beyond gender. The aim of this book has been to document and examine the variety of issues which feature in the politicisation of abortion, through the provision of a transnationally focused, interdisciplinary analysis of trends, illustrated using case studies from the Global North and South.

Within this book we very firmly position ourselves as feminist scholars from a range of disciplines (social policy, politics, medicine and women's studies), with a particular consciousness of abortion access as an issue of social justice. This is a strength of the analysis within the book. Our gaze is always firmly focused on outcomes for women in the society in which they live and the way that often abortion law and policy reflects wider gender inequalities within a particular society. As such, the study of abortion politics has much to tell us about power, gender inequality, attitudes towards women, healthcare provision, rights, the role of religion and conservative morality in lawmaking, both within particular societies and within emerging global trends.

There are a number of key points and arguments made within this book which are particularly important from a social justice perspective on abortion politics:

- The criminalisation of abortion continues to perpetuate a stigma about it as being wrong or against nature, or only justifiable under certain restricted parameters. It is clear that laws criminalising abortion fail to serve the purpose of either protecting women or preventing abortion. Abortion must be taken out of the criminal law, as its inclusion there fulfils no necessary or proportionate function and serves only to perpetuate archaic and conservative notions towards women and their agency.

- Biomedicalisation has changed access to abortion and the relationship between abortion seekers and health professionals. Pharmaceutical companies have in some cases had noble motives for developing abortifacients, while others have been tempered with the influence of commercial pressures and political framing of the state. While the abortion pill is, if used properly, largely safe, the majority of the risk-taking in the biomedicalisation of abortion has been shouldered by women in restricted settings, who are forced to access abortion medication through informal suppliers or established organisations such as Safe2Choose, Women on Web and Women Help Women. Although abortion medication has allowed women greater autonomy over the abortion process, it has also been limited by overregulation and a paternalistic approach to healthcare.

- Religious ideologies and cultural norms and discourses influence abortion policymaking, with both conservative and liberal perspectives influencing international and national policy. Religious, national and cultural discourses can be utilised as a means both to stifle legal change and to continue stigmatisation, which often leads to unsafe abortion practices and in fact higher rates of abortion in the particular state. The complexity of the utilisation of such discourses in societies emerging from transition identifies that opportunities for reform vary between settings and implementation of reform is often constrained if underlying cultural norms remain hostile to abortion.

- Globally, all states are bound by the various human rights treaties they are signatories to. As Chapter Five notes, abortion access can be linked with a number of human rights issues, including privacy, inhumane or degrading treatment, liberty and equality. While until very recently an international human rights framework on improving access to abortion has been elusive, increasingly human rights bodies are establishing at least minimum standards for abortion access, if not clearly articulating the right to abortion without restriction. As such, while international bodies are limited in terms of sanctions, collectively they can, and should continue to, contribute to external pressure on a state to invoke reform.

- Record numbers of people are affected by conflict and crisis. In such situations there is a need to ensure that women have access to reproductive health care. Sexual and reproductive health rights and services have been marginal within crisis interventions by the international community, with non-state actors often providing services. Organisations such as IPPF and its local partners have played a significant role in addressing this, providing access to basic services, all within a restricted funding environment. This is particularly the case since the reintroduction of the Global Gag Rule, which removes US funding from any organisation that 'performs or actively promotes abortion as a method of family planning' overseas. In this current climate, the development of services and ring-fencing of funding for these specific crisis interventions is fundamental.

• The politicisation of abortion has been responded to by a legion of dedicated, highly skilled activists. A range of organisations that operate transnationally, often collaborating with grassroots organisations, work to share knowledge, skills and learning, and to provide resources to those most affected by restrictive laws and limited access to abortion. The internet has enabled sharing and connection transnationally, and has helped facilitate the solidarity that comes from realising that abortion is an issue for almost all societies.

• Throughout the writing of this book, the authors have come on a journey in their own reading of abortion politics. In particular, we have increasingly engaged more with the developing concept of reproductive justice in our own work and writing. We hope the reader, in engaging with the final substantive chapter of this book, can also begin to conceptualise abortion in relation to other reproductive injustices that women face globally and the role of intersecting identities, whether that be race, class, ethnicity or sexuality, in policy and lawmaking responses.

The ideas explored in this study are situated in differing contexts around the globe: in countries where gender equality is relatively normalised and in countries where gender equality appears far from reach; in countries where abortion rights are regressing, and countries were abortion rights are widening; in countries emerging from conflict, and those that have been peaceful; in countries where health systems are well funded, and countries with poor health infrastructures. Most importantly, there appears to be few countries in the world where abortion is depoliticised and there are no issues with either the law surrounding abortion or with access to abortion.

We have identified a series of overarching themes that we view as guiding attitudes towards abortion and the law and policy which defines it: morality, lived experience, framings of abortion rights and changing trends in access. Consequently, we pose the question: where do we go from here?

Where do we go from here?

Morality

Our analysis exposes the resonances between the religious right and conservative forces and their attempt to assert a monopoly on morality. We argue that the positioning of abortion as a moral issue needs to be reclaimed: unsafe abortion results in thousands of deaths of women and girls every year; thousands more injuries are incurred; families suffer bereavement; lives are forever changed. To ignore this is obscene. We assert that denying access to abortion is immoral. This debate on morality, while dominated by the Christian right and its contentious grasp and understanding of morality, is being challenged by liberal faith-based organisations, demonstrating that the moral authority claimed by the right can be challenged from within the faith sector. This reclaiming of morality speaks to earlier analysis by Petchesky (1996: 328), who argued that a historical amnesia exists regarding the moral discourse surrounding abortion, with a lack of understanding that this discourse is socially constructed and not static.

Lived experience

Abortion is a subject around which a powerful mythology has been created. This mythology asserts that women suffer physical and mental injury from abortion. It implies that if abortion is illegal it won't happen, and that the majority of people in society oppose abortion. These are all falsehoods disproven by fact and academic evidence. However, one of the most powerful facilitators for change in abortion attitudes is lived experience. While factual evidence serves as a basis for challenging stigma, stereotype and myth, exposure to lived experience (either through one's own experience or by listening to someone else's) has the potential to fundamentally alter people's views on abortion. We assert that sharing lived experience has incredible transformative potential for the politicisation of abortion, and that social movements and activists have a pivotal role to play here:

> When shared reality biases are held firmly by the powerful, contentious politics are often necessary to induce large numbers of people to re-examine deeply entrenched norms. Social movements are one method for waging contentious politics, providing a powerful social practice for the peaceful transformation of moral consciousness, and undermining

the moral authority of those in power. (this publication, Chapter Six: 88)

We must be cognisant too of the burden placed on those telling their stories, to ensure they are supported in sharing it.

Framings of abortion rights

This book has presented a number of arguments and framings of abortion rights, moving from decriminalisation through human rights, healthcare access, cultural discourses and finally the concept of reproductive justice. We recognise that some framings are more successful than others, both globally and within local contexts. We argue that for the future of abortion access activism to be inclusive and diverse, an increasing focus must take account of the concept of reproductive justice, which recognises the right to abortion and the right to parent. Such an approach allows for a multilayered analysis taking account of poverty, race, ethnicity, age, sexuality, (dis)ability, citizenship and other identities which can be impacted in different ways by policies and laws governing reproduction.

Changing trends in abortion access and activism

Within this book we have detailed the changes that technology has brought to abortion access. This can be seen both in relation to abortion procedures and medication, and with regard to abortion activism. The biomedicalisation of abortion, for instance, has led to the relationship with health providers changing and a move away from clinical settings, and has provided greater opportunities for abortion services to be conducted by a range of health providers, not just medics. In addition, it is evident that the changes mean that abortion is being self-procured by women who have difficulties in accessing abortion through traditional care routes. These changes present two points for consideration. First, with more readily accessible abortion medication, we may see abortion moving out of the public political realm and back towards the private sphere. This move is bound to be preceded by a variety of backlashes intending to ensure control over women's bodies and reproductive lives. Second, while changes in accessing abortion present an opportunity in some contexts for women to access what they are unable to access otherwise, we cannot give up on the ideal that abortion should be provided as a public health service within a well-run, well-funded, comprehensive and equitable healthcare system.

Finally, we acknowledge that technology has also allowed activists to connect more quickly with women in need of abortion access and provide them with abortion pills, blurring the lines between healthcare and traditional activism activities.

In conclusion, it appears that each time there is a means to make abortion more accessible, either through law and policy or healthcare provisions, it is accompanied by a further politicisation of abortion which attempts to restrict this accessibility. Each time this happens, activists, healthcare providers and women who need abortion access mobilise in an attempt to reclaim their right to access what is often a relatively normal and routine healthcare procedure. Part of the aim of this book has been to uncover the forms that this politicisation takes, and to analyse and explain them, and we hope to provide understanding of how and why control of women's reproductive lives continues to be a very tightly held rein.

References

Aiken, A. R., Scott, J. G., Gomperts, R., Trussell, J., Worrell, M. and Aiken, C. E. (2016) 'Requests for abortion in Latin America related to concern about Zika virus exposure', *New England Journal of Medicine,* 375(4): 396–8.

Aiken, A. R., Digol, I., Trussell, J. and Gomperts, R. (2017a) 'Self reported outcomes and adverse events after medical abortion through online telemedicine: population based study in the Republic of Ireland and Northern Ireland', *bmj,* https://doi.org/10.1136/bmj.j2011

Aiken, A. R., Gomperts, R. and Trussell, J. (2017b) 'Experiences and characteristics of women seeking and completing at-home medical termination of pregnancy through online telemedicine in Ireland and Northern Ireland: a population-based analysis,' *BJOG: An International Journal of Obstetrics and Gynaecology,* 124(8): 1208–15.

Aiken, A. R., Guthrie, K. A., Schellekens, M., Trussell, J. and Gomperts, R. (2017c) 'Barriers to accessing abortion services and perspectives on using mifepristone and misoprostol at home in Great Britain' *Contraception,* https://doi.org/10.1016/j.contraception.2017.09.003

Amnesty International (2007) 'Amnesty International defends access to abortion for women at risk', press release, Amnesty International, https://www.amnesty.org/download/Documents/68000/pol300122007en.pdf

Amnesty International (2016) 'Amnesty International Campaign Roundup, My Body My Rights', https://www.amnesty.org.uk/files/my_body_my_right_-_roundup.pdf

Amy, J. J. and Rowlands, S. (2018) 'Legalised non-consensual sterilisation – eugenics put into practice before 1945, and the aftermath. Part 1: USA, Japan, Canada and Mexico', *The European Journal of Contraception and Reproductive Health Care,* https://doi.org/10.1080/13625187.2018.1450973.

Anderson, E. (2014) *Social movements, experiments in living, and moral progress: Case studies from Britain's abolition of slavery,* the Lindley Lecture, University of Kansas, 11 February 2014, http://williamstarr.net/workshop16/mckinney2.pdf

ARK (2017) *Northern Ireland Life and Times Survey, 2016* [computer file], ARK [distributor] www.ark.ac.uk/nilt

Bart, P. B. (1987) 'Seizing the means of reproduction: an illegal feminist abortion collective – how and why it worked', *Qualitative Sociology,* 10(4): 339–57.

Berer, M., Shah, I. and AbouZahr, C. (2016) 'A call for consensus and cooperation to resolve differing estimates of abortion-related deaths', *International Journal of Gynecology and Obstetrics*, 135(2): 127–8.

Black, R. (2015) 'Gay marriage vote exposes deep divisions within Northern Ireland parties', *Belfast Telegraph,* 28 April.

Blofield, M. (2008) 'Women's choices in comparative perspective: abortion policies in late-developing Catholic countries', *Comparative Politics*, 40(4): 399–419.

Bloomer, F. (2013) 'Protests, parades and marches: activism and extending abortion legislation to Northern Ireland' in L. Fitzpatrick (ed) *Performing feminisms in contemporary Ireland,* Dublin: Carysfort Press, pp 245–65.

Bloomer, F. and Fegan, E. (2014) 'Critiquing recent abortion law and policy in Northern Ireland', *Critical Social Policy*, 34(1): 109–20.

Bloomer, F. and O'Dowd, K. (2014) 'Restricted access to abortion in the Republic of Ireland and Northern Ireland: exploring abortion tourism and barriers to legal reform', *Culture, Health and Sexuality: An International Journal for Research, Intervention and Care*, 16(4): 366–80.

Bloomer, F. and Pierson, C. (2016) *Morality policy under the lens: evidence based policy making on abortion versus myth-usage*, briefing paper, Northern Ireland Assembly, www.niassembly.gov.uk/globalassets/documents/raise/knowledge_exchange/briefing_papers/series6/bloomer161116.pdf

Bloomer, F., McNeilly, K. and Pierson, C. (2016) *Moving forward from judicial review on abortion in situations of fatal foetal abnormality and sexual crime: The experience of health professionals*, Briefing paper, Reproductive Health Law and Policy Advisory Group, https://reproductivehealthlawpolicy.files.wordpress.com/2017/03/healthcareprofessionalsroundtablereport-090916.pdf

Bloomer, F., McNeilly, K. and Pierson, C. (2017a) *Northern Ireland overview of monitoring data on abortions*, briefing paper, Reproductive Health Law and Policy Advisory Group, https://reproductivehealthlawpolicy.files.wordpress.com/2017/03/monitoring-data-on-abortion-2017.pdf

Bloomer, F., Devlin-Trew, J., Pierson, C., MacNamara, N. and Mackle, D., (2017b) *Abortion as a workplace issue: Trade union survey – North and South of Ireland*, Dublin: UNITE the Union, Unison, Mandate Trade Union, the CWU Ireland, the GMB, Alliance for Choice, Trade Union Campaign to Repeal the 8th.

Bloomer, F., McQuarrie, C., Pierson, C. and Stettner, S. (2018a) 'Introduction', in C. McQuarrie, F. Bloomer, C. Pierson and S. Stettner (eds) *Abortion in anti-choice islands: Crossing troubled waters*, Prince Edward Island: Island Studies Press, pp ii–xxi.

Bloomer, F., McNeilly, K. and Pierson, C. (2018b) *Report of the inquiry concerning the United Kingdom of Great Britain and Northern Ireland under article 8 of the Optional Protocol to the Convention on the Elimination of All Forms of Discrimination against Women*, Briefing paper, Reproductive Health Law and Policy Advisory Group, https://reproductivehealthlawpolicy.files.wordpress.com/2018/04/cedaw-briefing-rhlpag4.pdf

Boland, R. and Katzive, L. (2008) 'Developments in laws on induced abortion: 1998–2007', *International Family Planning Perspectives*, 34(3): 110–20.

Bowater, F. (2015) Abortion in Brazil: a matter of life and death, *The Observer*, 1 February 2015, www.theguardian.com/world/2015/feb/01/abortion-in-brazil-a-matter-of-life-and-death

Briozzo, L., Vidiella, G., Rodríguez, F., Gorgoroso, M., Faúndes, A. and Pons, J. E. (2006) 'A risk reduction strategy to prevent maternal deaths associated with unsafe abortion', *International Journal of Gynecology and Obstetrics*, 95(2): 221–6.

Briozzo, L., Gómez Ponce de León, R., Tomasso, G. and Faúndes, A. (2016) 'Overall and abortion-related maternal mortality rates in Uruguay over the past 25 years and their association with policies and actions aimed at protecting women's rights', *International Journal of Gynecology and Obstetrics*, 134(S1): S20–S23.

British Medical Association (2017) *Decriminalisation of abortion: A discussion paper from the BMA*, London: BMA.

Brubaker, R. (2012) 'Religion and nationalism: four approaches', *Nations and nationalism*, 18(1): 2–20.

Bunreacht na hÉireann (1937) *Constitution of Ireland*, Dublin: Stationery Office.

Busza, J. and Lush, L. (1999) 'Planning reproductive health in conflict: a conceptual framework' *Social Science and Medicine*, 49: 155–171.

California State Auditor (2014) *Sterilization of female inmates: Some inmates were sterilized unlawfully, and safeguards designed to limit occurrences of the procedure failed: Report 2013-120*, Sacramento: California State Auditor.

Campbell, D. (2016) Abortion rate in England and Wales hits five-year high, *The Guardian*, 17 May 2016, https://www.theguardian.com/world/2016/may/17/abortion-rate-england-and-wales-five-year-high

Campbell, E. and Clancy, S. (2018) 'From grassroots to government: engagement strategies in abortion access activism in Ireland', in C. McQuarrie, F. Bloomer, C. Pierson and S. Stettner (eds) *Abortion in anti-choice islands: Crossing troubled waters*, Prince Edward Island: Island Studies Press, pp 204–34.

Catholic Bishops' Conference in the Philippines (CBCP) (2000) *That they may have life and have it abundantly*, Manila: Catholic Bishops' Conference in the Philippines.

CEDAW (1999) *Concluding observations on the fifth periodic report of the United Kingdom of Great Britain and Northern Ireland*, Geneva: United Nations.

CEDAW (2013) *Concluding observations on the seventh periodic report of the United Kingdom of Great Britain and Northern Ireland*, Geneva: United Nations.

CEDAW (2015) *Summary of the inquiry concerning the Philippines under article 8 of the Optional Protocol to the Convention on the Elimination of All Forms of Discrimination against Women: Committee on the Elimination of Discrimination against Women*, Geneva: United Nations.

CEDAW (2016) *Concluding observations on the combined seventh and eighth periodic reports of the Philippines: Committee on the Elimination of Discrimination against Women*, Geneva: United Nations.

CEDAW (2018) *Report of the inquiry concerning the United Kingdom of Great Britain and Northern Ireland under article 8 of the Optional Protocol to the Convention on the Elimination of All Forms of Discrimination against Women*, Geneva: United Nations.

Center for Reproductive Rights (CRR) (2008) *Case challenging Manila contraception ban dismissed*, New York: Center for Reproductive Rights.

Center for Reproductive Rights (CRR) (2015) *Accountability for discrimination against women in the Philippines: Key findings and recommendations from the CEDAW Committee's Special Inquiry on Reproductive Rights*, New York: Center for Reproductive Rights.

Center for Reproductive Rights (CRR) (2018) *World abortion laws*, http://worldabortionlaws.com

Central Statistics Office (2011) *Census data*, Dublin: Central Statistics Office.

Charo, R. A. (1991) 'A political history of RU-486', in K. E. Hanna (ed) *Biomedical politics*, Washington, DC: The National Academies Press.

Chong, A. and Troy, J. (2011) 'A universal sacred mission and the universal secular organization: the Holy See and the United Nations', *Politics, Religion and Ideology*, 12(3): 335–54.

Clarke, A. and Montini, T. (1993) 'The many faces of RU486: tales of situated knowledges and technological contestations', *Science, Technology, and Human Values*, 18(1): 42–78.

Clarke, A. E., Mamo, L., Fosket, J. R., Fishman, J. R. and Shim, J. K. (eds) (2009) *Biomedicalization: Technoscience, Health, and Illness in the US*, Durham, NC: Duke University Press.

Clements, B. (2014) 'Religion and the sources of public opposition to abortion in Britain: the role of "belonging", "Behaving" and "Believing"', *Sociology*, 48(2): 369–86.

Cockrill, K. and Nack, A. (2013) '"I'm not that type of person": managing the stigma of having an abortion', *Deviant Behavior*, 34(12): 973–90.

Commission for Gender Equality (2014) *Beyond the numbers: Mainstreaming gender in the public service*, Johannesburg: Commission for Gender Equality, www.cge.org.za/wp-content/uploads/2014/05/Gender-Barometer-2014.pdf

Cook, R. J. (2000) 'Developments in abortion laws: comparative and international perspectives', *Annals of the New York Academy of Sciences*, 913(1): 74–87.

Coomaraswamy, R. (1994) *Preliminary report submitted by the Special Rapporteur on Violence against Women, Its Causes and Consequences*, New York: United Nations Economic and Social Council.

Costa, S. H. and Vessey, M. P. (1993) 'Misoprostol and illegal abortion in Rio de Janeiro, Brazil', *The Lancet*, 341(8855): 1258–61.

Crenshaw, K. (1991) 'Mapping the margins: intersectionality, identity politics, and violence against women of color', *Stanford Law Review*, 43(6): 1241–99.

Cresswell, T. (2010) 'Towards a politics of mobility', *Environment and Planning* 28(1): 17–31.

Danco (2016) 'Mifeprex® (mifepristone): FDA approves updated labeling', www.earlyoptionpill.com/wp-content/uploads/2016/03/Mifeprex-Label-Update_Press-Release_March302016.pdf

de Londras, F. and Enright, M. (2018) *Repealing the 8th: Reforming Irish abortion law*, Bristol: Policy Press.

de Londras, F. and Markicevic, M. (2018) 'Reforming abortion law in Ireland: Reflections on the public submissions to the Citizens' Assembly', *Women's Studies International Forum*, https://doi.org/10.1016/j.wsif.2018.08.005

De Zordo, S. D. (2016) 'The bio-medicalisation of illegal abortion: the double life of Misoprostol in Brazil', *História, Ciências, Saúde-Manguinhos*, 23(1): 19–36.

Debbink, M. L., Hassinger, J. A., Martin, L. A., Maniere, E., Youatt, E. and Harris, L. H. (2016) 'Experiences with the providers share workshop method: abortion worker support and research in tandem', *Qualitative health research*, 26(13): 1823–37.

Demeterio-Melgar, J.L., Linangan ng Kababaihan, Reproductive Health, Rights, Ethics and Center for Studies and Training, Center for Reproductive Rights (2007) *Imposing misery: The impact of Manila's ban on contraception*, Quezon City: Likhaan.

Department of Health (England) (2018) *Abortion statistics, England and Wales: 2017*, London: Department of Health.

Department of Health (Republic of Ireland) (2016) *Second annual report of notifications in accordance with the Protection of Life during Pregnancy Act, 2013*, Press release, http://health.gov.ie/blog/press-release/second-annual-report-of-notifications-in-accordance-with-the-protection-of-life-during-pregnancy-act-2013

Department for International Development (UK) (2013) *Safe and Unsafe Abortion: The UK's policy position on safe and unsafe abortion in developing countries*, London: DFID.

Diniz, S. G., d'Oliveira, A.F.P.L. and Lansky, S. (2012) 'Equity and women's health services for contraception, abortion and childbirth in Brazil', *Reproductive Health Matters*, 20(40): 94–101.

Diniz, D., Medeiros, M. and Madeiro, A. (2017) 'National Abortion Survey 2016', *Ciência and Saúde Coletiva*, 22(2): 653–60.

Dixon-Mueller, R. (1988) 'Innovations in reproductive health care: menstrual regulation policies and programs in Bangladesh', *Studies in Family Planning*, 19(3): 129–40.

Dlamini, B. (2014) 'The ANC's approach to abortion', www.politicsweb.co.za/documents/the-ancs-approach-to-abortion--bathabile-dlamini

Dudley, J. (2011) *Broken words: The abuse of science and faith in American politics*, New York: Crown.

Duffy, D. and Pierson, C. (2017) 'What happens when women have to travel: abortion, care and lessons from Ireland', *Metropolis*, https://mcrmetropolis.uk/blog/what-happens-when-women-have-to-travel-abortion-care-and-lessons-from-ireland/

Durham, M. (2005) 'Abortion, gay rights and politics in Britain and America: a comparison', *Parliamentary Affairs*, 58(1): 89–103.

Eig, J. (2016) *The birth of the pill: How four pioneers reinvented sex and launched a revolution*, London: Pan Macmillan.

Engeli, I. (2012) 'Policy struggle on reproduction: doctors, women, and Christians', *Political Research Quarterly*, 65(2): 330–45.

Engeli, I., Green-Pedersen, C. and Larsen, L. T. (2013) 'The puzzle of permissiveness: understanding policy processes concerning morality issues', *Journal of European Public Policy*, 20(3): 335–52.

Englehart, N. A. and Miller, M. K. (2014) 'The CEDAW effect: international law's impact on women's rights', *Journal of Human Rights*, 13(1): 22–47.

Enright, M. (2017) *#Strike4Repeal: Ireland's Women's Strike*, http://criticallegalthinking.com/2017/03/08/strike4repeal-irelands-womens-strike/

Erdman, J. N. (2018) 'The bridge of abortion's constitutional return and future', in C. McQuarrie, F. Bloomer, C. Pierson and S. Stettner (eds) *Abortion in anti-choice islands: Crossing troubled waters*, Prince Edward Island: Island Studies Press, pp 105–16.

ESCR-Net (2015) *Committee on the Elimination of Discrimination against Women (CEDAW) Inquiry concerning the Philippines (CEDAW/C/OP.8/PHL/1)*, New York: International Network for Economic, Social and Cultural Rights, https://www.escr-net.org/caselaw/2015/committee-elimination-discrimination-against-women-cedaw-inquiry-concerning-philippines

Estrada-Claudio, S. (2010a) 'Sanctifying moral tyranny: religious fundamentalisms and the political disempowerment of women', in C. Derichs and A. Fleschenberg (eds) *Religious fundamentalisms and their gendered impacts in Asia*, Berlin: Friedrich-Ebert, Stiftung.

Estrada-Claudio, S. (2010b) 'The International Women and Health Meetings: deploying multiple identities for political sustainability', in P. Dufour, D. Masson and D. Caouette (eds) *Solidarities beyond borders: Transnationalizing women's movements*, Vancouver: UBC Press, pp 108–26.

Evans, D. (2013) *Sexual citizenship: The material construction of sexualities*, Abingdon: Routledge.

Farid, S. (2016) 'Does Egypt's new tourist marriage law really protect women?', *Al Arabiya News*, 18 January 2016.

FDA (Bureau of Food and Drug Administration Philippines) (2002) *BFAD Advisory No. 02-02 || MISOPROSTOL (CYTOTEC): Unregistered Drug Product*.

Fine, J. B., Mayall, K. and Sepúlveda, L. (2017) 'The role of international human rights norms in the liberalization of abortion laws globally', *Health and Human Rights*, 19(1): 69–79.

Finer, L. and Fine, J. B. (2013) 'Abortion law around the world: progress and pushback', *American Journal of Public Health*, 103(4): 585–9.

Fisher, K. (1998) 'Women's experience of abortion before the 1967 Abortion Act: a study of South Wales c. 1930–1950', in E. Lee (ed) *Abortion law and politics today*, Basingstoke: Macmillan.

Fitzgerald, J. M., Krause, K. E., Yermak, D., Dunne, S., Hannigan, A., Cullen, W., Meagher, D., McGrath, D., Finucane, P., Coffey, C. and Dunne, C. (2014) 'The first survey of attitudes of medical students in Ireland towards termination of pregnancy', *Journal of Medical Ethics*, 40(10): 710–13.

Fletcher, R. (2013) 'Peripheral governance: administering transnational health-care flows', *International Journal of Law in Context*, 9(2): 160–91.

FPA, Alliance for Choice and NIWEP (2010) *Submission of evidence to the CEDAW Committee Optional Protocol: Inquiry procedure*, Belfast: FPA.

Galli, B. (2016) *Abortion rights in Brazil: A big step forward*, Ipas, www.ipas.org/en/News/2016/December/Abortion-rights-in-Brazil-A-big-step-forward.aspx

Ganiel, G. (2006) 'Ulster says maybe: the restructuring of evangelical politics in Northern Ireland', *Irish Political Studies*, 21(2): 137–55.

Gerber Fried, M. (2013) 'Reproductive rights activism in the post-Roe era', *American Journal of Public Health*, 103(1): 10–14.

Gerber Fried, M., Ross, L. and Solinger, R. (2013) 'Understanding reproductive justice: a response to O'Brien', *Rewire*, 8 May 2013, https://rewire.news/article/2013/05/08/understanding-reproductive-justice-a-response-to-obrien

Gerdts, C., Fuentes, L., Grossman, D., White, K., Keefe-Oates, B., Baum, S. E., Hopkins, K., Stolp, C. W. and Potter, J. E. (2016) 'Impact of clinic closures on women obtaining abortion services after implementation of a restrictive law in Texas', *American Journal of Public Health*, 106(5): 857–64.

Geronimo J. Y. (2016) 'DOH readies case vs Sorsogon mayor for "gross violation" of RH law', *Rappler*, 22 June 2016, https://www.rappler.com/nation/137269-doh-case-sorsogon-city-mayor-violation-rh-law

Gianella, C., Rodriguez de Assis Machado, M. and Peñas Defago, A. (2017) *What causes Latin America's high incidence of adolescent pregnancy?* (CMI Brief vol. 16, no. 9), Bergen: Chr. Michelsen Institute.

Gold, M. and Chong, E. (2015) 'If we can do it for misoprostol, why not for mifepristone? The case for taking Mifepristone out of the office in medical abortion', *Contraception*, 92(3): 194–6.

Gomperts, R. J., Jelinska, K., Davies, S., Gemzell-Danielsson, K. and Kleiverda, G. (2008) 'Using telemedicine for termination of pregnancy with mifepristone and misoprostol in settings where there is no access to safe services', *BJOG: An International Journal of Obstetrics and Gynaecology*, 115(9): 1171–8.

Government of the Arab Republic of Egypt and United National Population Fund (2013) *Country Programme Action Plan between the Government of Egypt and UNFPA 2013–2017*, Cairo: Government of the Arab Republic of Egypt and United National Population Fund.

Government of South Africa (1996) *Choice on Termination of Pregnancy Act, Act 92*, Cape Town: South African Government Gazette, www.gov.za/sites/www.gov.za/files/Act92of1996.pdf

Government of Sweden (2016) *Swedish Foreign Service action plan for feminist foreign policy 2015–2018*, Government Offices of Sweden: Ministry for Foreign Affairs.

Government of Sweden (2018) *Handbook: Sweden's Feminist Foreign Policy*, Government Offices of Sweden: Ministry for Foreign Affairs.

Gray, A. M. (2017) *Attitudes to abortion in Northern Ireland: ARK Research Update 115*, www.ark.ac.uk/publications/updates/update115.pdf

Gray, A. M. and Birrell, D. (2012) 'Coalition government in Northern Ireland: social policy and the lowest common denominator thesis', *Social Policy and Society,* 11(1): 15–25.

Greenhouse, S. (1989) 'New pill, a fierce battle', *New York Times*, 12 February 1989, www.nytimes.com/1989/02/12/magazine/a-new-pill-a-fierce-battle.html?pagewanted=1

Gresh, A. and Maharaj, P. (2014) 'Termination of pregnancy: perspectives of female students in Durban, South Africa', *Etude de la Population Africaine*, 28(1): 681–90.

Grimes, D. A., Benson, J., Singh, S., Romero, M., Ganatra, B., Okonofua, F. E. and Shah, I. H. (2006) 'Unsafe abortion: the preventable pandemic', *The Lancet*, 368(9550): 1908–19.

Grossman, D. and Grindlay, K. (2017) 'Safety of medical abortion provided through telemedicine compared with in person', *Obstetrics and Gynecology*, 130(4): 778–82.

Grossman, D., Constant, D., Lince, N., Alblas, M., Blanchard, K. and Harries, J. (2011) 'Surgical and medical second trimester abortion in South Africa: a cross-sectional study', *BMC Health Services Research*, 11(1): 224–33.

Guns, W. (2013) 'The influence of the feminist anti-abortion NGOs as norm setters at the level of the UN: contesting UN norms on reproductive autonomy, 1995–2005', *Human Rights Quarterly*, 35(3): 673–700.

Guttmacher Institute (2013) *Unintended pregnancy and unsafe abortion in the Philippines*, New York: Guttmacher Institute, https://www.guttmacher.org/fact-sheet/unintended-pregnancy-and-unsafe-abortion-philippines

Guttmacher Institute (2017a) *Policy brief: In a state of crisis: Meeting the sexual and reproductive health needs of women in humanitarian situations*, New York: Guttmacher Institute, https://www.guttmacher.org/gpr/2017/02/state-crisis-meeting-sexual-and-reproductive-health-needs-women-humanitarian-situations

Guttmacher Institute (2017b) *Menstrual regulation and unsafe abortion in Bangladesh*, New York: Guttmacher Institute, https://www.guttmacher.org/fact-sheet/menstrual-regulation-unsafe-abortion-bangladesh

Haddad, L. B. and Nour, N. M. (2009) 'Unsafe abortion: unnecessary maternal mortality', *Reviews in Obstetrics and Gynecology*, 2(2): 122–6.

Hajri, S., Blum, J., Gueddana, N., Saadi, H., Maazoun, L., Chelli, H., Dabash, R. and Winikoff, B. (2004) 'Expanding medical abortion in Tunisia: women's experiences from a multi-site expansion study', *Contraception*, 70(6): 487–91.

Hansard (2013) *Official report of the Northern Ireland Assembly, Tuesday 12 March 2013*, Volume 83, no. 2, Belfast: Northern Ireland Assembly.

Harper, C. C., Blanchard, K., Grossman, D., Henderson, J. T. and Darney, P. D. (2007) 'Reducing maternal mortality due to elective abortion: potential impact of misoprostol in low-resource settings', *International Journal of Gynecology and Obstetrics*, 98(1): 66–9.

Harris, L. H., Martin, L., Debbink, M. and Hassinger, J. (2013) 'Physicians, abortion provision and the legitimacy paradox', *Contraception*, 87(1): 11–16.

Hayes, B. C. and Dowds, L. (2010) 'Religion and attitudes towards gay rights in Northern Ireland: the God gap revisited', in S. E. Brunn (ed) *The changing world religion map*, Dordrecht: Springer.

Hendrickson, C., Fetters, T., Mupeta, S., Vwallika, B., Djemo, P. and Raisanen, K. (2016) 'Client–pharmacy worker interactions regarding medical abortion in Zambia in 2009 and 2011', *International Journal of Gynecology and Obstetrics*, 132: 214–18.

Hessini, L. (2016) 'Reclaiming and reframing sexual rights in Muslim-majority contexts: the role of individual and collective movements in shifting patriarchal discourse and practice', The *Brown Journal of World Affairs*, 22: 69–80.

Hodes, R. (2016) 'The culture of illegal abortion in South Africa', *Journal of Southern African Studies*, 42(1): 79–93.

Hodge, J. G., Corbett, A., Repka, A. and Judd, P. J. (2016) 'Zika virus and global implications for reproductive health reforms', *Disaster Medicine and Public Health Preparedness*, 10(5): 713–15.

Hoggart, L. (2012) '"I'm pregnant … what am I going to do?" An examination of value judgements and moral frameworks in teenage pregnancy decision making', *Health, Risk and Society*, 14: 533–49.

Hoggart, L. (2017) 'Internalised abortion stigma: young women's strategies of resistance and rejection', *Feminism and Psychology*, 27(2): 186–202.

Hoggart, L., Newton, V. L. and Bury, L. (2015) *How could this happen to me? Young women's experiences of unintended pregnancies: A qualitative study*, Milton Keynes: Open University Press.

Hoggart, L., Newton, V. L. and Bury, L. (2016) '"Repeat abortion", a phrase to be avoided? Qualitative insights into labelling and stigma', *Journal of Family Planning and Reproductive Health Care*, 43: 26–30.

Holland, K. (2014) 'Timeline of Ms Y case', *Irish Times*, 4 October 2014, https://www.irishtimes.com/news/social-affairs/timeline-of-ms-y-case-1.1951699

HSE (Health Service Executive) (2017) *Medical Cards*, available at https://www.hse.ie/eng/cards-schemes/medical-card/

Htun, M. and Power, T. J. (2006) 'Gender, parties, and support for equal rights in the Brazilian Congress', *Latin American Politics and Society*, 48(4): 83–104.

Huda, F. A., Ngo, T. D., Ahmed, A., Alam, A. and Reichenbach, L. (2014) 'Availability and provision of misoprostol and other medicines for menstrual regulation among pharmacies in Bangladesh via mystery client survey', *International Journal of Gynecology and Obstetrics*, 124: 164–8.

Hulme, D. (2009a) *The Millennium Development Goals (MDGs): A short history of the world's biggest promise*, Manchester: University of Manchester, Brooks World Poverty Institute.

Hulme, D. (2009b) *Politics, ethics and the Millennium Development Goals: The case of reproductive health*, BWPI Working Paper, Manchester: University of Manchester, Brooks World Poverty Institute.

Human Development Network (HDN) (2013) *2012–2013 Philippine Human Development Report*, www.hdn.org.ph/20122013-philippine-human-development-report

IAWG (2015) 'Reproductive health in the changing humanitarian context', http://iawg.net/wp-content/uploads/2016/08/IAWG-Global-Evaluation-2012-2014-1.pdf

IFPA (2016) 'Abortion in Ireland statistics', https://www.ifpa.ie/Hot-Topics/Abortion/Statistics

International Campaign for Women's Right to Safe Abortion (2015) 'International Safe Abortion Day global activities 2015', www. safeabortionwomensright.org/international-safe-abortion-day/ reports-from-day-of-action-28-sept-2015

International Campaign for Women's Right to Safe Abortion (2016) 'International Safe Abortion Day global activities 2016', www. safeabortionwomensright.org/international-safe-abortion-day/ international-safe-abortion-day-2016

International Campaign for Women's Right to Safe Abortion (2017a) 'Safe abortion information hotlines', www.safeabortionwomensright. org/safe-abortion-3/safe-abortion-information-hotlines

International Campaign for Women's Right to Safe Abortion (2017b) 'International Safe Abortion Day global activities 2017', www. safeabortionwomensright.org/international-safe-abortion-day/ international-safe-abortion-day-global-activities-2017

International Planned Parenthood Federation (IPPF) (2016) 'Plea for Aleppo', https://www.ippf.org/news/plea-aleppo

International Planned Parenthood Federation (IPPF) (2017) *'Policy briefing: The GGR and its impacts'*, https://www.ippf.org/sites/default/ files/2017-09/IPPF%20GGR%20Policy%20Briefing%20No.1%20 -%20August%202017.pdf

International Women's Health Coalition (2014) 'After victory in Uruguay: addressing gaps between the right to abortion and access to services', https://iwhc.org/2014/02/victory-uruguay-addressing-gaps-right-abortion-access-services

Ipas (2018) 'Just released: New Ipas toolkit to improve abortion access for refugee women and girls', http://www.ipas.org/ en/News/2018/June/Just-released-New-Ipas-toolkit-to-improve-abortion-access-for-refugee-women-and-girls. aspx?utm_source=AllListservs&utm_medium=listserve&utm_ content=read&utm_campaign=WorldRefugeeDay

Jackman, J. (2002) 'Anatomy of a feminist victory: winning the transfer of RU 486 patent rights to the United States, 1988–1994', *Women and Politics*, 24(3): 81–99.

Jackson, P. (1992) 'Abortion trials and tribulations', *The Canadian Journal of Irish Studies*, 18(1): 112–20.

Jaggar, A. M. (2014) *Gender and global justice*, Cambridge: Polity Press.

Jatlaoui, T. C., Ewing A., Mandel, M. G., Simmons, K. B., Suchdev, D. B., Jamieson, D. J. and Pazol, K. (2016) 'Abortion surveillance – United States, 2013', *MMWR Surveillance Summaries*, 65(SS-12): 1–44.

Jewkes, R. and Rees, H., (2008) 'Dramatic decline in abortion mortality due to the Choice on Termination of Pregnancy Act [letter]', *South African Medical Journal*, 95(4): 250.

Jilozian, A. and Agadjanian, V. (2016) 'Is induced abortion really declining in Armenia?', *Studies in Family Planning*, 47(2): 163–78.

Jimenez-David, R. (2011) 'Imposing their will', *Philippine Daily Inquirer*, 20 March, www.pressreader.com/philippines/philippine-daily-inquirer/20110320/283373353510262

Joffe, C. (1996) *Doctors of conscience: The struggle to provide abortion before and after Roe v. Wade*, Boston: Beacon Press.

Joffe, C. E. (2009) *Dispatches from the abortion wars: The costs of fanaticism to doctors, patients, and the rest of us*, Boston: Beacon Press.

Joffe, C. E., Weitz, T. A. and Stacey, C. L. (2004) 'Uneasy allies: pro-choice physicians, feminist health activists and the struggle for abortion rights', *Sociology of Health and Illness*, 26(6): 775–96.

Juarez, F., Cabigon, J., Singh, S. and Hussain, R. (2005) 'The incidence of induced abortion in the Philippines: current level and recent trends', *International Family Planning Perspectives*, 31(3): 140–9.

Kaplan, L. (1997) *The story of Jane: The legendary underground feminist abortion service*, Chicago, IL: University of Chicago Press.

Kassebaum, N. J., Bertozzi-Villa, A., Coggeshall, M. S., Shackelford, K. A., Steiner, C., Heuton, K. R. et al (2014) 'Global, regional, and national levels and causes of maternal mortality during 1990–2013: a systematic analysis for the Global Burden of Disease Study 2013', *Lancet* (384): 980–1004.

Kennedy, S. and Gilmartin, M. (2018) 'Mobility, migrants and abortion in Ireland', in C. McQuarrie, F. Bloomer, C. Pierson and S. Stettner (eds) *Abortion in anti-choice islands: Crossing troubled waters*, Prince Edward Island: Island Studies Press, pp 138–60.

Kennedy, R., Pierson, C. and Thomson, J. (2016) 'Challenging identity hierarchies: gender and consociational power-sharing', *The British Journal of Politics and International Relations*, 18(3): 618–33.

Kozlowska, I., Béland, D. and Lecours, A. (2016) 'Nationalism, religion, and abortion policy in four Catholic societies', *Nations and Nationalism*, 22(4): 824–44.

Kulczycki, A. (2011) 'Abortion in Latin America: changes in practice, growing conflict, and recent policy developments', *Studies in Family Planning*, 42(3): 199–220.

Kumar, A., Leila Hessini, L. and Mitchell, E.M.H. (2009) 'Conceptualising abortion stigma', *Culture, Health and Sexuality: An International Journal for Research, Intervention and Care*, 11(6): 625–39.

Lader, L. (1991) *RU 486: The pill that could end the abortion wars and why American women don't have it*, Reading, MA: Addison-Wesley.

Lara, D., Abuabara, K., Grossman, D. and Díaz-Olavarrieta, C. (2006) 'Pharmacy provision of medical abortifacients in a Latin American city', *Contraception*, 74(5): 394–9.

Lee, L. (2017) *Religion: Losing faith: British Social Attitudes, 28*, London: NatCen Social Research www.bsa.natcen.ac.uk/media/38958/bsa28_12religion.pdf

Lewis, H. (2003) 'Embracing complexity: human rights in critical race feminist perspective', *Columbia Journal of Gender and Law*, 12(3): 511–20.

Liebowitz, D. J. and Zwingel, S. (2014) 'Gender equality oversimplified: using CEDAW to counter the measurement obsession', *International Studies Review*, 16(3): 362–389.

Lipka, M. (2015) '5 facts about Catholicism in the Philippines', Washington, DC: Pew Research Center, www.pewresearch.org/fact-tank/2015/01/09/5-facts-about-catholicism-in-the-philippines

Macleod, C. I., (2018) 'Expanding reproductive justice through a supportability reparative justice framework: the case of abortion in South Africa', *Culture, Health and Sexuality: An International Journal for Research, Intervention and Care*, https://doi.org/10.1080/136910 58.2018.1447687

Macleod, C., Sigcau, N. and Luwaca, P. (2011) 'Culture as a discursive resource opposing legal abortion', *Critical Public Health*, 21(2): 237–45.

Macleod, C. I., Beynon-Jones, S. and Toerien, M. (2016) 'Articulating reproductive justice through reparative justice: case studies of abortion in Great Britain and South Africa', *Culture, Health and Sexuality: An International Journal for Research, Intervention and Care*, 19(5): 601–15.

Martins-Melo, F. R., Lima, M.D.S., Alencar, C. H., Ramos Jr, A. N., Carvalho, F.H.C., Machado, M.M.T. and Heukelbach, J. (2014) 'Temporal trends and spatial distribution of unsafe abortion in Brazil, 1996–2012', *Revista de Saúde Pública*, 48(3): 508–20.

McLaren, A. (1978) 'Abortion in France: women and the regulation of family size 1800–1914', *French Historical Studies*, 10(3): 461–85.

McMurtrie, S. M., García, S. G., Wilson, K. S., Diaz-Olavarrieta, C. and Fawcett, G. M. (2012) 'Public opinion about abortion-related stigma among Mexican Catholics and implications for unsafe abortion', *International Journal of Gynecology and Obstetrics*, 118: S160–66.

Medeiros, M., de Souza, P.H.G.F.D. and Castro, F.Á.D. (2015) 'The stability of income inequality in Brazil, 2006–2012: an estimate using income tax data and household surveys', *Ciência and Saúde Coletiva*, 20(4): 971–86.

Meintjes, S., Turshen, M. and Pillay, A. (2001) *The aftermath: Women in post-conflict transformation*, London: Zed Books.

Miller, S., Lehman, T., Campbell, M., Hemmerling, A., Brito Anderson, S., Rodriguez, H., Vargas Gonzalez, W., Cordero, M. and Calderon, V. (2005) 'Misoprostol and declining abortion-related morbidity in Santo Domingo, Dominican Republic: a temporal association', *BJOG: An International Journal of Obstetrics and Gynaecology*, 112(9): 1291–6.

Minkenberg, M. (2002) 'Religion and public policy: institutional, cultural, and political impact on the shaping of abortion policies in Western democracies', *Comparative Political Studies*, 35(2): 221–47.

Mishtal, J. (2016) 'Quietly "beating the system"', in S. De Zordo, J. Mishtal and L. Anton (eds) *A fragmented landscape: Abortion governance and protest logics in Europe*, New York: Berghan Books, pp 154–72.

Mitchell, C. (2006) *Religion, identity and politics in Northern Ireland: Boundaries of belonging and belief*, Aldershot: Ashgate.

Morgan, L. M. (2014) 'Claiming Rosa Parks: conservative Catholic bids for "rights" in contemporary Latin America', *Culture, Health and Sexuality: An International Journal for Research, Intervention and Care*, 16(10): 1245–59.

Morgan, L. M. (2015) 'Reproductive rights or reproductive justice? Lessons from Argentina', *Health and Human Rights: An International Journal*, 17(1): 136–47.

Mosley, E. A., King, E. J., Schulz, A. J., Harris, L. H., De Wet, N. and Anderson, B. A. (2017) 'Abortion attitudes among South Africans: findings from the 2013 social attitudes survey', *Culture, Health and Sexuality: An International Journal for Research, Intervention and Care*, 19(8): 918–33.

Murtagh C., Wells E., Raymond E. G., Coeytaux F., Winikoff, B. (2017) 'Exploring the feasibility of obtaining mifepristone and misoprostol from the internet', *Contraception*, https://doi: 10.1016/j.contraception.2017.09.016

Nakae, M. (2017) 'Reproductive justice issues for Asian and Pacific Islander women', www.protectchoice.org/article.php?id=134

Nash, E., Benson Gold, R., Mohammed, L., Cappello, O. and Ansari-Thomas, Z. (2017) *Laws affecting reproductive health and rights: State policy trends at midyear, 2017: policy pnalysis*, New York: Guttmacher Institute.

National Board of Health and Welfare (Sweden) (2016) 'Statistical database', www.socialstyrelsen.se/statistics/statisticaldatabase

Ngo, T. D., Park, M. H., Shakur, H. and Free, C. (2011) 'Comparative effectiveness, safety and acceptability of medical abortion at home and in a clinic: a systematic review', *Bulletin of the World Health Organization*, 89(5): 360–70.

O'Brien, J. (2013) 'Why we are and must remain "pro-choice"', *Rewire*, 25 April 2013, https://rewire.news/article/2013/04/25/why-we-are-and-must-remain-for-choice

O'Rourke, C. (2016) 'Advocating abortion rights in Northern Ireland: local and global tensions', *Social and Legal Studies*, 25(6): 716–40.

Office of the Mayor, Sorsogon City (2015) 'EO no 3: an executive order declaring Sorsogon City as a pro-life city', http://sorsogoncity.gov.ph/?issuance=eo-no-3-an-executive-order-declaring-sorsogon-city-as-a-pro-life-city

Oireachtas (2013) *Heads of Protection of Life during Pregnancy Bill 2013: Public hearings, Joint Committee on Health and Children, Friday 17 May 2013*, Dublin: Oireachtas.

Open Democracy (2011) '"Soft law" and hard choices: a conversation with Gita Sahgal, Open Democracy 50:50', https://www.opendemocracy.net/5050/deniz-kandiyoti/soft-law-and-hard-choices-conversation-with-gita-sahgal

Palmer, C. A. and Zwi, A. B. (1999) 'The emerging international policy agenda for reproductive health services in conflict settings', *Social Science and Medicine*, 49(12): 1689–1703.

Palmer, J. J. and Storeng, K. T. (2016) 'Building the nation's body: the contested role of abortion and family planning in post-war South Sudan', *Social Science and Medicine*, 168: 84–92.

Pan American Health Organization (World Health Organization Regional Office for the Americas) (2015) *Epidemiological alert: Increase of microcephaly in the northeast of Brazil*, https://www.paho.org/hq/index.php?option=com_content&view=article&id=11443%3A17-november-2015-increase-microcephaly-northeast-brazil-epidemiological-alert&catid=2103%3Arecent-epidemiological--alerts-updates&Itemid=42346&lang=en

Pan American Health Organization (World Health Organization Regional Office for the Americas) (2017) *Health in the Americas, Country Report Brazil – Country Report Brazil*, https://www.paho.org/salud-en-las-americas-2017/?page_id=97

Pangalangan R. (2015) 'Religion and the secular state: National report for the Philippines', in *religion and the secular states: Interim reports*, International Center for Law and Religion Studies, available at https://www.iclrs.org/index.php?blurb_id=975

Parker, W. (2017) *Life's work: a moral argument for choice*, New York: Simon and Schuster.

Pateman, C. (1988) *The sexual contract*, Palo Alto, CA: Stanford University Press.

Petchesky, R. P. (1986) *Abortion and woman's choice: The state, sexuality and reproductive freedom*, London: Verso.

Petroni, S. (2011) 'Historical and current influences on United States international family planning policy', *Journal of Women, Politics and Policy*, 32(1): 28–51.

Philippine Statistics Authority (PSA) (2015) *Philippines in Figures 2015*, Quezon City: Philippine Statistics Authority.

Philippine Statistics Authority (PSA) (2017) 'Farmers, fishermen and children consistently posted the highest poverty incidence among basic sectors', (reference no: 2017-150, https://psa.gov.ph/poverty-press-releases

Pierson, C. and Bloomer, F. (2017) 'Macro-and micro-political vernacularizations of rights: human rights and abortion discourses in Northern Ireland', *Health and Human Rights*, 19(1): 173–86.

Politi, D. (2018) 'Legal abortion in Argentina? A long shot is suddenly within reach', *New York Times*, 14 April 2018, https://www.nytimes.com/2018/04/14/world/americas/argentina-abortion-pope-francis.html

PopCom (2017) Population Growth Slows as Contraceptive Use Spikes. Manila: Commission on Population Philippines, www.popcom.gov.ph/about-us/10-press-releases/484-population-growth-slows-as-contraceptive-use-spikes-2

Powell-Jackson, T., Acharya, R., Filippi, V. and Ronsmans, C. (2015) 'Delivering medical abortion at scale: a study of the retail market for medical abortion in Madhya Pradesh, India', *PloS One*, 10(3): 1–14.

Purcell, C., Cameron, S., Lawton, J., Glasier, A. and Harden, J. (2017) 'The changing body work of abortion: a qualitative study of the experiences of health professionals', *Sociology of Health and Illness*, 39(1): 78–94.

Rahman, A., Katzive, L. and Henshaw, S. K. (1998) 'A global review of laws on induced abortion, 1985–1997', *International Family Planning Perspectives*, 24(2): 56–64.

Ramos, S., Romero, M. and Aizenberg, L., (2014) 'Women's experiences with the use of medical abortion in a legally restricted context: the case of Argentina', *Reproductive Health Matters*, 22(suppl. 44): 4–15.

Raymond, J. G., Klein, R. and Dumble, L. J. (1991) *RU486: Misconceptions, myths and morals*, Cambridge, MA: Institute on Women and Technology.

Rebouche, R. (2016) 'How radical is reproductive justice? Remarks for the FIU Law Review Symposium', *FIU Law Review*, 12(9): 9–25.

Reiss, K., Footman, K., Akora, V., Liambila, W. and Ngo, T. D. (2016) 'Pharmacy workers' knowledge and provision of medication for termination of pregnancy in Kenya', *Journal of Family Planning and Reproductive Health Care*, 42: 208–12.

RESURJ, ANIS, Columbia University Mailman School of Public Health (2015a) *Evidence and justice: Brazil*, http://resourcecenter. resurj.org/pages/view.php?ref=127

RESURJ, EIPR, Columbia University Mailman School of Public Health (2015b) *Evidence and justice: Making the case for adolescent health and rights, Egypt 2015*, http://resourcecenter.resurj.org/pages/view. php?ref=128

Riddle, J. M. (1999) *Eve's herbs: A history of contraception and abortion in the West*, Cambridge, MA: Harvard University Press.

Roberts, D. E. (2017) *Killing the black body: Race, reproduction, and the meaning of liberty* (2nd edn), New York: Vintage Books.

Rose, M. (2007) *Safe, legal, and unavailable? Abortion politics in the United States*, Washington, DC: Congressional Quarterly Press.

Ross, L. (2011) 'Fighting the black anti-abortion campaign: Trusting black women', *On The Issues Magazine*, Winter 2011, www. ontheissuesmagazine.com/2011winter/2011_winter_Ross.php

Ross, L. and Solinger, R. (2017) *Reproductive justice: An introduction* (vol. 1), Oakland, CA: University of California Press.

Ross, L. J., Brownlee, S. L., Diallo, D. D., Rodriguez, L. and Roundtable, L., (2001) 'The "SisterSong collective": women of color, reproductive health and human rights', *American Journal of Health Studies*, 17(2): 79–88.

Rufo, A. C. (2013) *Altar of secrets*, Manila: Journalism for Nation Building Foundation.

Samsara (2017) 'Rekomendasi', http://askinna.com/jangan-mau-ditipu-penjual-obat-penipu

Say, L., Chou, D., Gemmill, A., Tunçalp, Ö., Moller, A. B., Daniels, J., Gülmezoglu, A. M., Temmerman, M. and Alkema, L. (2014) 'Global causes of maternal death: a WHO systematic analysis', *The Lancet Global Health*, 2(6): e323–33.

Schwartz, M. A. and Tatalovich, R. (2009) 'Cultural and institutional factors affecting political contention over moral issues', *Comparative Sociology*, 8(1): 76–104.

Sedgh, G., Bearak, J., Singh, S., Bankole, A., Popinchalk, A., Ganatra, B., Rossier, C., Gerdts, C., Tunçalp, Ö., Johnson, B. R. and Johnston, H. B. (2016) 'Abortion incidence between 1990 and 2014: global, regional, and subregional levels and trends', *The Lancet*, 388 (10041): 216–17.

Sedgh, G., Singh, S., Henshaw, S. K. and Bankole, A. (2011) 'Legal abortion worldwide in 2008: levels and recent trends', *Perspectives on Sexual and Reproductive Health*, 43(3): 188–98.

Seidman, G. (1999) 'Is South Africa different? Sociological comparisons and theoretical contributions from the land of apartheid', *Annual review of sociology*, 25(1): 419–40.

Sethna, C. and Doull, M. (2012) 'Accidental tourists: Canadian women, abortion tourism, and travel', *Women's Studies*, 41(4): 457–75.

Sheldon, S. (2016) 'How can a state control swallowing? The home use of abortion pills in Ireland', *Reproductive Health Matters*, 24(48): 90–101.

Sherris, J., Bingham, A., Burns, M. A., Girvin, S., Westley, E. and Gomez, P. I. (2005) 'Misoprostol use in developing countries: results from a multicountry study', *International Journal of Gynecology and Obstetrics*, 88(1): 76–81.

Silliman, J., Ross, L., Gutiérrez, E. and Gerber Fried, M. (2016) *Undivided rights: Women of color organizing for reproductive justice*, Chicago, IL: Haymarket Books.

Simonds, W., Ellertson, C., Winikoff, B. and Springer, K. (2001) 'Providers, pills and power: the US mifepristone abortion trials and caregivers' interpretations of clinical power dynamics', *Health*, 5(2): 207–31.

Singh, S., Monteiro, M. F. and Levin, J. (2012) 'Trends in hospitalization for abortion-related complications in Brazil, 1992–2009: Why the decline in numbers and severity?', *International Journal of Gynecology and Obstetrics*, 118: S99–106.

Smith, A. (2015) *Conquest: Sexual violence and American Indian genocide*, Durham, NC: Duke University Press.

Solinger, R. (1996) *The abortionist: A woman against the law*, Berkley, CA: University of California Press.

Supreme Court (Republic of the Philippines) (2014) G.R. Nos. 217872 and 221866, http://sc.judiciary.gov.ph/pdf/web/viewer.html?file=/ jurisprudence/2016/august2016/217872.pdf

Tamang, A., Puri, M., Masud, S., Karki, D. K., Khadka, D., Singh, M., Sharma, P. and Gajurel, S. (2017) 'Medical abortion can be provided safely and effectively by pharmacy workers trained within a harm reduction framework: Nepal', *Contraception*, https://doi. org/10.1016/j.contraception.2017.09.004

Tanabe, M., Myers, A., Bhandari, P., Cornier, N., Doraiswamy, S. and Krause, S. (2017) 'Family planning in refugee settings: findings and actions from a multi-country study', *Conflict and Health*, *11*(1): 9–23.

Taylor, R. (2009) *Consociational theory: McGarry and O'Leary and the Northern Ireland conflict*, Abingdon: Routledge.

Teffo, M. E. and Rispel, L. C. (2017) '"I am all alone": factors influencing the provision of termination of pregnancy services in two South African provinces', *Global Health Action*, 10(1), https:// doi.org/10.1080/16549716.2017.1347369

Thomson, J. (2018) 'A "United" Kingdom? The 1967 Abortion Act and Northern Ireland', in C. McQuarrie, F. Bloomer, C. Pierson and S. Stettner (eds) *Abortion in anti-choice islands: Crossing troubled waters*, Prince Edward Island: Island Studies Press, pp 161–83.

Thomson, J. and Pierson, C. (2018) 'Can abortion rights be integrated into the Women, Peace and Security agenda?' *International Feminist Journal of Politics*, https://doi.org/10.1080/14616742.2017.1413583

Tonge, J., Braniff, M., Hennessey, T., McAuley, J. W. and Whiting, S. (2014) *The Democratic Unionist Party: From protest to power*, Oxford: Oxford University Press.

Trueman, K. A. and Magwentshu, M. (2013) 'Abortion in a progressive legal environment: the need for vigilance in protecting and promoting access to safe abortion services in South Africa', *American Journal of Public Health*, 103(3): 397–9.

UNCAT (2006) Consideration of Reports Submitted by State Parties Under Article 19 of the Convention: Conclusions and recommendations of the Committee against Torture, Peru, UN Doc. CAT/C/PER/CO/4, at para. 23.

UNCESRC (2000) General Comment on Article 12, General Comment No. 14 UN CESCR Comm. Econ., Soc. and Cultural Rts., 22nd Sess., UN Doc. E/C.12/2000/4 (2000), at para 30.

UNCESRC (2005) General Comment No. 16 UN CESCR Comm. Econ, Soc and Cultural Rights., 34th Sess. UN Doc. E/C. 12/2005/ 4 (2005), at para. 29.

UNHRC (2000) CCPR General Comment No. 28: Article 3 (The Equality of Rights Between Men and Women), 29 March 2000, CCPR/C/21/Rev.1/Add.10.

UNICCPR (2012) Concluding observations on the fourth periodic report of the Philippines, UN Human Rights Committee, 106th sess. UN Doc. CCPR/C/PHL/CO/4 at para. 13.

UNOCHA (2017) Office for the Coordination of Humanitarian Affairs: Annual Report 2017, https://www.unocha.org/sites/unocha/files/2017%20annual%20report.pdf

UN Security Council (2013) Resolution on sexual violence in conflict, S/RES/2106.

Verdeja, E. (2008) 'A critical theory of reparative justice', *Constellations*, 15(2): 208–22.

Viana, M. and Gumieri, S. (2016) *'Poor Brazilian women carry the greater burden of the Zika virus epidemic'*, http://resurj.org/node/58

Victora, C. G., Aquino, E. M., do Carmo Leal, M., Monteiro, C. A., Barros, F. C. and Szwarcwald, C. L. (2011) 'Maternal and child health in Brazil: progress and challenges', *The Lancet*, 377(9780): 1863–76.

Warriner, I. K., Wang, D., Huong, N. M., Thapa, K., Tamang, A., Shah, I., Baird, D. T. and Meirik, O. (2011) 'Can midlevel health-care providers administer early medical abortion as safely and effectively as doctors? A randomised controlled equivalence trial in Nepal', *The Lancet*, 377(9772): 1155–61.

Waylen, G. (2010) 'Gendering politics and policy in transitions to democracy: Chile and South Africa', *Policy and Politics*, 38(3): 337–52.

Weeks, A. D., Fiala, C. and Safar, P. (2005) 'Misoprostol and the debate over off-label drug use', *BJOG: An International Journal of Obstetrics and Gynaecology*, 112(3): 269–72.

WHO (2003) *Safe Abortion: Technical and policy guidance for health systems*, Geneva: World Health Organization.

WHO (2011) *Unsafe abortion: Global and regional estimates of the incidence of unsafe abortion and associated mortality in 2008* (6th edn), Geneva: World Health Organization.

WHO (2012) *Safe abortion: Technical and policy guidance for health systems* (2nd edn), Geneva: World Health Organization.

WHO (2014) *Clinical practice handbook for safe abortion*, Geneva: World Health Organization.

WHO (2016) 'Maternal mortality in 1990–2015: Brazil', www.who.int/gho/maternal_health/countries/bra.pdf?ua=1

WHO (2017a) *Model list of essential medicines*, (20th edition), www.who.int/medicines/publications/essentialmedicines/en

WHO (2017b) 'Country profile: South Africa', African Regional Office, www.who.int/countries/zaf/en

Williams, D. K. (2013) 'No happy medium: the role of Americans' ambivalent view of fetal rights in political conflict over abortion legalization', *Journal of Policy History*, 25(1): 42–61.

Wilson, K. S., Garcia, S. G. and Lara, D. (2010) 'Misoprostol use and its impact on measuring abortion incidence and morbidity', in S. Singh, L. Lisa Remez and A. Tartaglione (eds) *Methodologies for estimating abortion incidence and abortion-related morbidity: A review'*, New York: Guttmacher Institute, pp 191–201.

Winn, P. (2017) 'Inside the Philippines' women-run crime ring selling abortion elixirs', *Global Post Investigations*, 23 August 2017, https://gpinvestigations.pri.org/inside-the-philippines-women-run-crime-ring-selling-abortion-elixirs-51cd2de6cb8b

Women Help Women (2017) 'Using abortion pills for safe abortion in the US: self-managed abortion: safe and supported (SASS)',https://abortionpillinfo.org/en/using-abortion-pills-for-safe-abortion-usa

Women on Web (2017) 'Warning, fake abortion pills for sale online!! False medicines offered for sale!', www.womenonwaves.org/en/page/974/warning--fake-abortion-pills-for-sale-online

Wood, S., Abracinskas, L., Correa, S. and Pecheny, M. (2016) 'Reform of abortion law in Uruguay: context, process and lessons learned', *Reproductive Health Matters*, 24(48): 102–10.

Wulf, D. (1994) *Refugee women and reproductive health: Reassessing priorities*, New York: Women's Commission for Refugee Women and Children.

Yuval-Davis, N. (1997) *Gender and nation*, London: Sage.

Zamberlin, N., Romero, M. and Ramos, S. (2012) 'Latin American women's experiences with medical abortion in settings where abortion is legally restricted', *Reproductive Health*, 9(34): 1–12.

Zampas, C. (2016) 'Legal and political discourses on women's right to abortion', in S. De Zordo, J. Mishtal and L. Anton (eds) *A fragmented landscape: Abortion governance and protest logics in Europe*, New York: Berghan Books, pp 20–32.

Zampas, C. and Gher, J. M. (2008) 'Abortion as a human right: international and regional standards', *Human Rights Law Review*, 8(2): 249–94.

Zurbriggen, R., Keefe-Oates, B. and Gerdts, C. (2017) 'Accompaniment of second-trimester abortions: the model of the feminist Socorrista network of Argentina', *Contraception*, https://doi.org/10.1016/j.contraception.2017.07.170

Index

NOTE: Page numbers in italic type refer to figures.